Street by Street

SOUTHPORT
FORMBY, ORMSKIRK, SKELMERSDALE

Ainsdale, Aughton Park, Banks, Bescar, Birkdale, Burscough Bridge, Churchtown, Hightown, Scarisbrick, Up Holland

2nd edition November 2007
© Automobile Association Developments Limited 2007

Original edition printed April 2002

This product includes map data licensed from Ordnance Survey® with the permission of the Controller of Her Majesty's Stationery Office. © Crown copyright 2007. All rights reserved. Licence number 100021153.

The copyright in all PAF is owned by Royal Mail Group plc.

Published by AA Publishing (a trading name of Automobile Association Developments Limited, whose registered office is Fanum House, Basing View, Basingstoke, Hampshire RG21 4EA. Registered number 1878835).

Produced by the Mapping Services Department of The Automobile Association. (A03390)

A CIP Catalogue record for this book is available from the British Library.

Printed by Oriental Press in Dubai

The contents of this atlas are believed to be correct at the time of the latest revision. However, the publishers cannot be held responsible or liable for any loss or damage occasioned to any person acting or refraining from action as a result of any use or reliance on any material in this atlas, nor for any errors, omissions or changes in such material. This does not affect your statutory rights. The publishers would welcome information to correct any errors or omissions and to keep this atlas up to date. Please write to Publishing, The Automobile Association, Fanum House (FH12), Basing View, Basingstoke, Hampshire, RG21 4EA. E-mail: streetbystreet@theaa.com

Ref: ML202z

Key to map pages	ii-iii
Key to map symbols	iv-1
Enlarged map pages	2-3
Main map pages	4-41
Index – towns & villages	42
Index – streets	43-49
Index – featured places	49-50
Acknowledgements	50

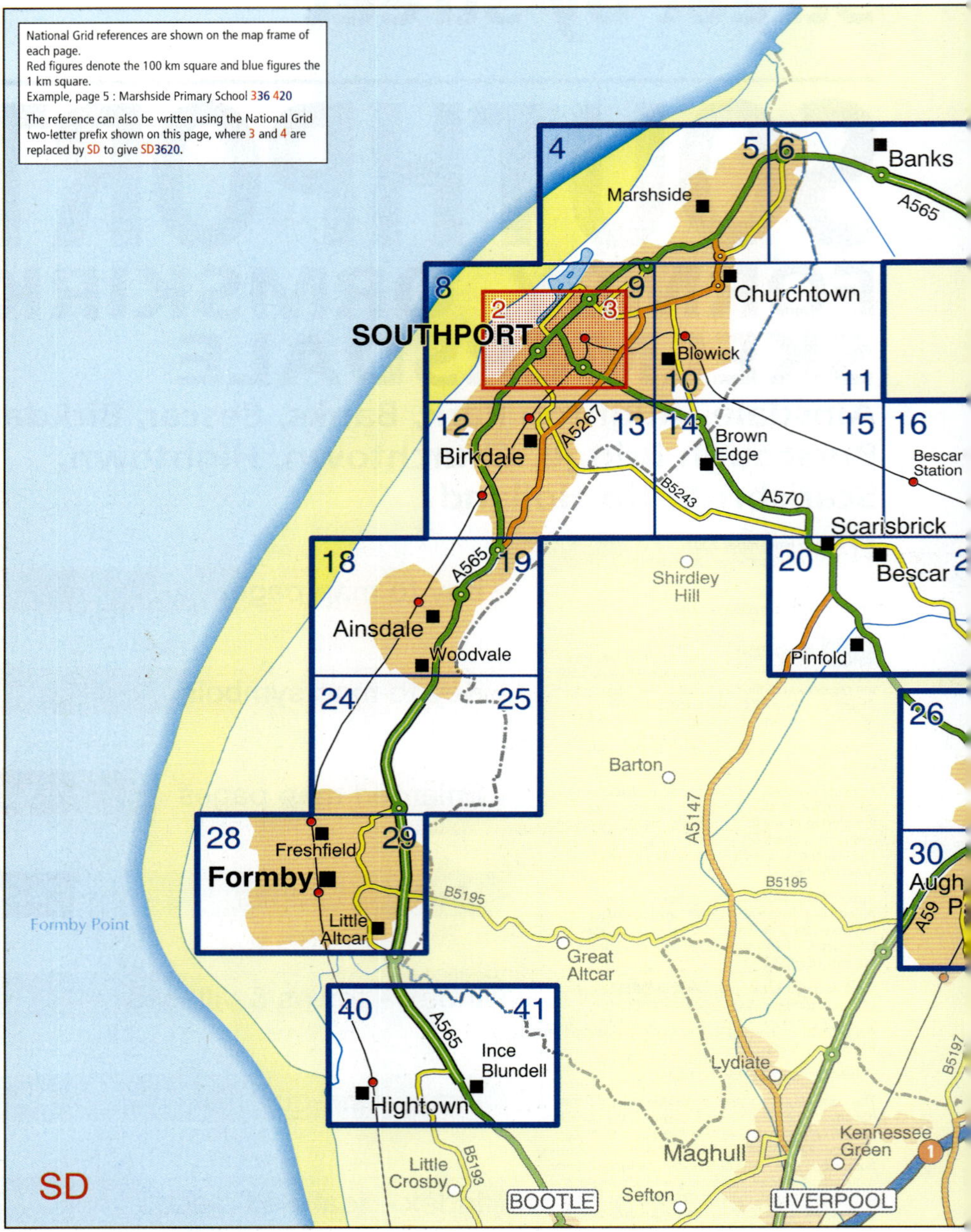

National Grid references are shown on the map frame of each page.
Red figures denote the 100 km square and blue figures the 1 km square.
Example, page 5 : Marshside Primary School 336 420

The reference can also be written using the National Grid two-letter prefix shown on this page, where 3 and 4 are replaced by SD to give SD3620.

4

Marshside

5 **6**
Banks

A565

8 **9**
Churchtown

2 **3**

SOUTHPORT

Blowick

10

11

12 **13** **14**
Birkdale

Brown Edge

A5267

B5243

15 **16**

Bescar Station

A570

Scarisbrick

18 **19**
Ainsdale

Woodvale

A565

Shirdley Hill

20
Bescar

Pinfold

24 **25**

Barton

A5147

26

28 **29**
Freshfield

Formby

Little Altcar

B5195

B5195

Great Altcar

30
Augh...
P...

A59

40 **41**
Ince Blundell

A565

Hightown

Lydiate

B5197

Little Crosby

B5193

Maghull

Kennessee Green

1

BOOTLE

Sefton

LIVERPOOL

SD

Formby Point

Enlarged scale pages   **1:10,000**   6.3 inches to 1 mile

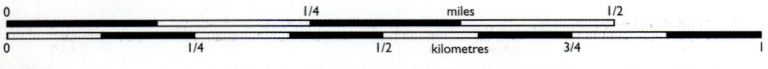

0   1/4   miles   1/2

0   1/4   1/2   kilometres   3/4   1

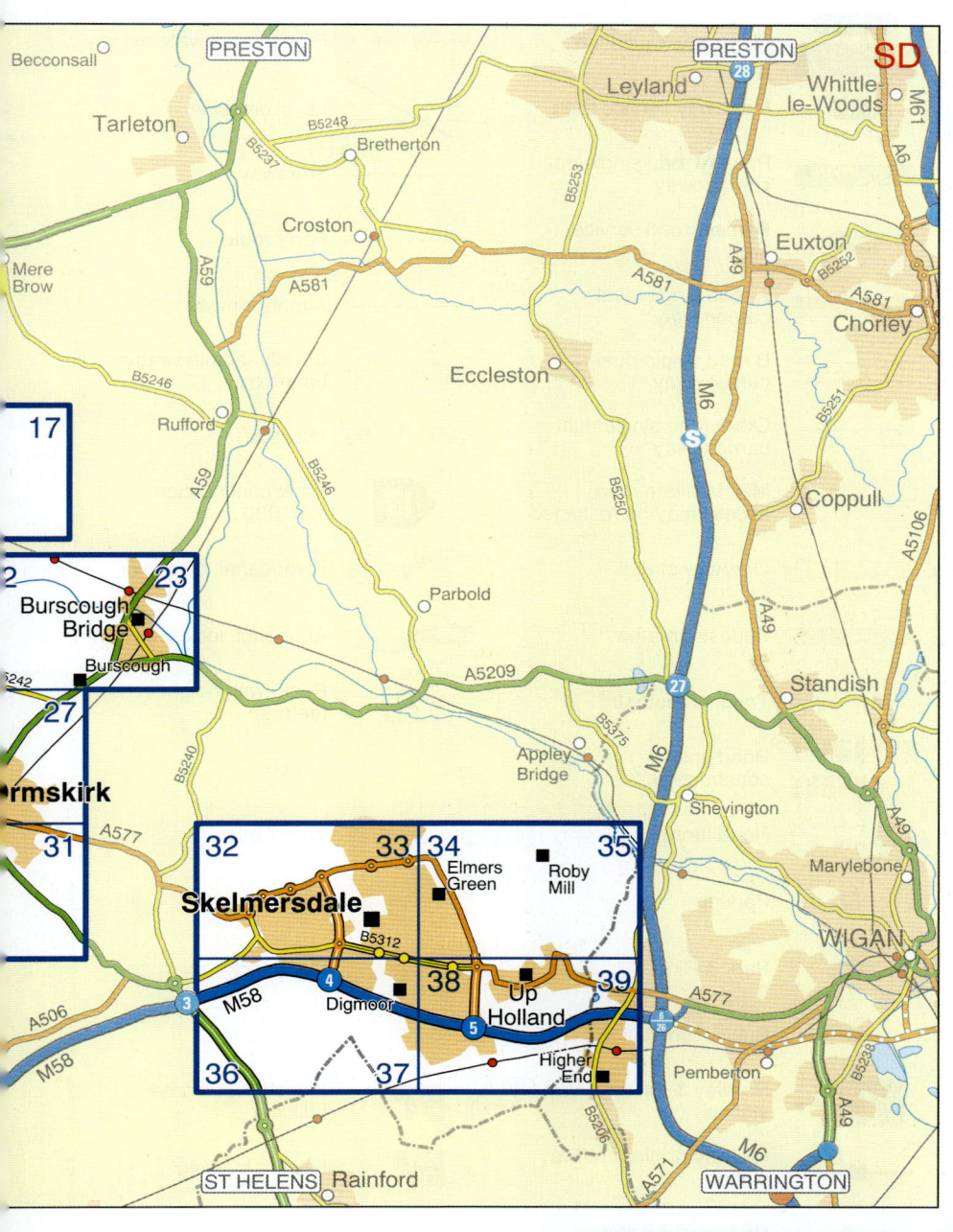

Junction 9	Motorway & junction	++++++++++	Preserved private railway
Services	Motorway service area	LC	Level crossing
	Primary road single/dual carriageway	●—●—●—●	Tramway
Services	Primary road service area	- - - - - -	Ferry route
	A road single/dual carriageway	....	Airport runway
	B road single/dual carriageway	- · — · — · —	County, administrative boundary
	Other road single/dual carriageway	vvvvvvvvvvv	Mounds
	Minor/private road, access may be restricted	17	Page continuation 1:15,000
← ←	One-way street		River/canal, lake, pier
	Pedestrian area		Aqueduct, lock, weir
- - - - - - -	Track or footpath	465 ▲ Winter Hill	Peak (with height in metres)
	Road under construction		Beach
[- - - =]	Road tunnel		Woodland
P	Parking		Park
P+	Park & Ride		Cemetery
	Bus/coach station		Built-up area
	Railway & main railway station		Industrial/business building
	Railway & minor railway station		Leisure building
⊖	Underground station		Retail building
⊖	Light railway & station		Other building

City wall			Castle	
A&E	Hospital with 24-hour A&E department		Historic house or building	
PO	Post Office		Wakehurst Place (NT)	National Trust property
	Public library		Museum or art gallery	
i	Tourist Information Centre		Roman antiquity	
i	Seasonal Tourist Information Centre		Ancient site, battlefield or monument	
	Petrol station, 24 hour Major suppliers only		Industrial interest	
†	Church/chapel		Garden	
	Public toilets		Garden Centre Garden Centre Association Member	
	Toilet with disabled facilities		Garden Centre Wyevale Garden Centre	
PH	Public house AA recommended		Arboretum	
	Restaurant AA inspected		Farm or animal centre	
Madeira Hotel	Hotel AA inspected		Zoological or wildlife collection	
	Theatre or performing arts centre		Bird collection	
	Cinema		Nature reserve	
	Golf course		Aquarium	
▲	Camping AA inspected		Visitor or heritage centre	
	Caravan site AA inspected		Country park	
	Camping & caravan site AA inspected		Cave	
	Theme park		Windmill	
	Abbey, cathedral or priory		Distillery, brewery or vineyard	

2

SOUTHPORT

Southport Pier

Premier Travel Inn

Model Village

Pleasureland

Marine Drive

Esplanade

Southport Swimming Baths

Victoria Way

Southport Flower Show Site

Superstore

Duke St

Beach Priory Gdns

Priory Mews

LORD ST WEST

Rotten Row

Beechfield Gardens

Sunnymede School

Castle Walk

Beach Rd

A565

Works

St Paul's Str

Westcliffe Road

Kingswood Park

Southern Road

Hollybro Road

Southport Landing Area

Esplanade

Rotten Row

Blandford Close

Warren Ct

Palatine Road

ROAD

AUGHTON ROAD

Twistfield Close

Gloucester

Amberley Se Road

Ascot Cl

Ascot Cl

Weld

Westcliffe Road

ELWORTH

Saxon

Road

k Road

1 grid square represents 250 metres

A   B   8   C   D   E

I

2

3

8

4

5

6

7

A   B   8   C   D   E

3 32   18

33

4 17

3 32   33

4

A   B   C   D

3 33   34

21

I

2

20

3

Marshside
Sands

Marshside RSPB
Reserve

4

419

5

Golf Course

Hesketh Road

Marine Drive

P

3 33   34

Southport
Municipal
Golf Club

A   B   **9**   C   D

PARK

Marine Lake

Pro

Albany Road

Leyland Road

Lathom Road

Avondale Road N

Park Road West

Fleetwood Road

Cliff Rd

Argyle

Fairway

Hesketh
Centre
(Hospital)

PARK ROAD

P

I grid square represents 500 metres

Southport

A B C D

331 32

I

18

2

SOUTHPORT

Southport
Pier

Marine Drive

P

Pleasurela

3

17

Marine
Drive

P

Esplanac

Victoria Way

P+

Southport Flower
Show Site

Beechdale
Gdns

4

Southport
Landing Area

Marine
Drive

Esplanade

Sunnymede
School

Row

Beech
Rd

Rotten

Kingswood
Park

A565

Blandford
Close

Warren

Westcliffe

Palatine
Road

Cl

5

2

416

331 32

A B **12** C D

Camberley
Cl

Palace Road

Ascot
Close

Weld

Westcliffe
Ct

Grovewood

Oxford
Gardens

Oxford

LULWORTH ROAD

Saxon Road

Prince Charles Gdns

Westbourne
Gardens

Windsor
Court

Road

Carnoustie
Cl

Phory
Gardens

Victoria
Court

Canterbury

Birk
Sta

Y

Chase
Close

Regen

Westbourne

E F **6** G H

38

39

I

2

3

17

4

5

416

E F **15** G H

38

39

Three Pools W

Lane

Dolly's Lane

New Lane

Long

Beanygate

Winacre
Farm

Dolly's

Lane

Moss Lane

Straight Up La

Moss Lane

Wyke Hey
Farm

Wyke Lane

Wyke Wood Lane

Wyke House
Farm

Perch Pool Lane

Wyke Lane

The

Avenue

Wyke Thorn
Farm

h Pool Lane

Wyke
Lane

12

16

3 3 1

A **B** **8** **C** **D**
32

I

Camberley Cl
Palace Road
Ascot Close
Westcliffe
Weld
Grovewood
LULWORTH ROAD
Saxon Road
Prince charles Gdns
Priory Gardens
Canterbury
Victoria Court
Birk
Stati
Bickerton Rd
Chase
Close

Westbourne
Road

Westbourne Gardens

Oxford Road
Oxford Gdns
Windsor Court
Regent Close
Regent Road
Regency Gdns
Regent Ms
Nelson Ct
Treesdale Close
Sunnyside

Westbourne

Granville Road
Lancaster
Lancaster Close
Grosvenor
Rl Pk?
Grosvenor Road
Grosvenor Close
Belgrave Rd
Broadlands
Worthing Close
Dover Rd
Crosb
Sull
Clos

Selworthy Road

Sandringham Road
Selworthy
Gainsborough Road
Trafalgar
Churchfields
Cricket Pch
Southport & Birkdale CC
Burlington
Cres

2

15

Coastal Road

Selworthy

Harrod Drive
LC
Conyers Av
Stan

Breeze Road
Sherringham Road
Cromer Road
Dover Drive
Blundell Av
Carlton Lawn Tennis Club
Blundell Drive
Dunkirk Road
Hartley Road
Richm

3

Greenbank Drive
Trafalgar Road
Blundell Cts
Kirkstall Rd
Clive
Clv Ldg
Birk Trac Esta

Hillside

Hillside Station

Grinstead Cl
St Joh

The Royal Birkdale Golf Club
Golf Course

Greenbank High Sch

Wtrh Rd
Dunbar
Kirklees Rd
Cardigan Road
Carna
Rd

4

4 1 4

Coastal Road

Hillside Golf Club

Hastings Road
Lynton Drive
Sandon Road
Ashton Rd
Langdale Gardens
Norfolk Gv

Hillside Golf Club
Road
Southport RFC
Arundel Road
Dunbar Crescent
Woodstock Drive

5

Lynton Road
Clovelly Drive
Dunbar Crescent
LIVERPOOL
Far

Dunster Road
Ryder Crescent

Golf Course

A **B** **19** **C** **D**
3 3 1 32

Windy Harbour Road
Carr Lane
PR

Birkdale High School
bourne Av
Ranelag
Dr

A565

I grid square represents 500 metres

E F 11 G H

38 39

Wyke Thorn Farm

16

Perch Pool Lane

I

Wyke Lane

LC Pool Hey Lane

Shaw's Farm

2

LC

Wyke Cop Road

15

Woodmoss Lane

3

Wyke Road Farm

16

Woodmoss Lane

Pinewood Close

Greenfield Road

w Hall ve

4

Hares Lane

Snape Green

Rimmer Green

Cat Tall Lane

A570

SOUTHPORT ROAD

Snape Gn

414

Besca ne

5

Carr Cross

Sandy Brook

Hillcrest Drive

39

Woodland Avenue

LANE

St Marks CE Primary School

38

20

Culshaw Close

B5242

Besca

E F 20 G H

Hooton's Farm

Scarisbrick

SCAR BROW LANE

Sweart Close

Clyffes Farm

Clyffes Close

St Marys RC

16

A   B   C   D

Midge Hall Farms

Caunce's Road

3 39   **40**

16

1

Wyke Wood Lane

15

2

Greenings Lane

Greenings

Midge Hall Lane

Wholesome Lane

3

15

Perch Pool Lane

Bescar Lane

Bescar Lane Station

LC

Woodmoss Lane

4

†

PO

Drummersdale Lane

White House Lane

414

Copelands

White Hous

5

Bescar Lane

Hillcrest Drive

3 39   **40**

A   B   **21**   C   D

Bescar

B5242

Culshaw WY

Everard Close

Besc Brw La

Hillock Lane

Hillock Close

Highfield Lane

rsdale Lane

Cliffes Farm

St Marys RC

1 grid square represents 500 metres

Whams Farm

E

F

G

H

42

43

I

Berry House

Berry House Road

Windmill Animal Farm

Wholesome Lane

Fish Lane

2

15

3

Wildfowl & Wetlands Trust Martin Mere

4

14

LC

5

Martin Lane

LC

42

43

E

F

G

H

New Lane

Marsh Moss Lane

Marsh Moss House

New Lane

16

18

A   B   C   D

3 29   30

1

13

2

Sands

Ainsdale

3

12

4

Ainsdale-on-Sea

5

4 11

3 29   30

Shore Rd

Promenade

Shore Road

Coastal Road

Chiltern Road

Chatswort

Chatsworth Rd

Petworth Road

Chatwell Rd

Chatstock Dr

Blenheim

Tavistock Dr

Tudor Rd

Daneway

Greyfriars Road

Shore

stratford Close

Barford Close

Arden Cl

Grafton Dr

Ettington

Harvington Drive

Broadway Cl

McK Cl

Daresbury Avenue

Prestbury Av

Chipping Av

Chandley Close

Barrington Dr

Kettering Rd

Delamere Road

Mandeville Road

North Dr

Leach Dr

Alder

dale

Arlington Close

Brinklow Close

Sevenoaks Avenue

Rothwell Dr

Sambourn Fold

Meriden Cl

Rothley Av

Westminster

Bosworth Dr

Wilmcote Cv

Lighthorne Dr

Cantlow Fold

Kingsbury Cl

Drive

Shoreside Primary School

Pershore Cv

Shelton Dr

Harbury

Quinton Cl

Wigton Cl

Avenue

Merefield Special School

Mardale Close

Easedale

Kendal Way

Woodside Av

Sunbu

Midhurs

Furness

Thirlmere Drive

Drive

Newby

Coastal Road

Pinfold Lane

Woodv

Pinfold

Willowbank Holida
Home & Touring P

Ainsdale S   Dunes
National N   Reserve   **A**   **B**   **24**   **C**   **D**

I grid square represents 500 metres

20

A   B   15   C   D

ACKSMERE   LANE

3 37   38

St Ma CE
Primary School

Scarisbrick

Sandy Brook

Woodland
Avenue

Hillcrest
Drive

B5242

Culs
W

Evesard
Close
e e

1

Hooton's Farm

Southport
Rd

Southport

BESCAR BROW LANE

Bullens
Lane

A570

Dr

13

Black

Mancha

2

Moss   Lane

SOUTHPORT ROAD

Police
Station

3

Renacres Hall
Hospital

12

A5147

GORSUCH LANE

A570

SOUTHPORT ROAD

Renacres Lane

4

Pinfold

Halsall Moss

5

Leeds & Liverpool Canal

Morris   Lane

Pinfold
Lane

Gr   Lane

3 37   38

A   B   C   D

ROAD

Hulmes Bridge
Business Centre

Small Lane North

North Moor

Grange

1 grid square represents 500 metres

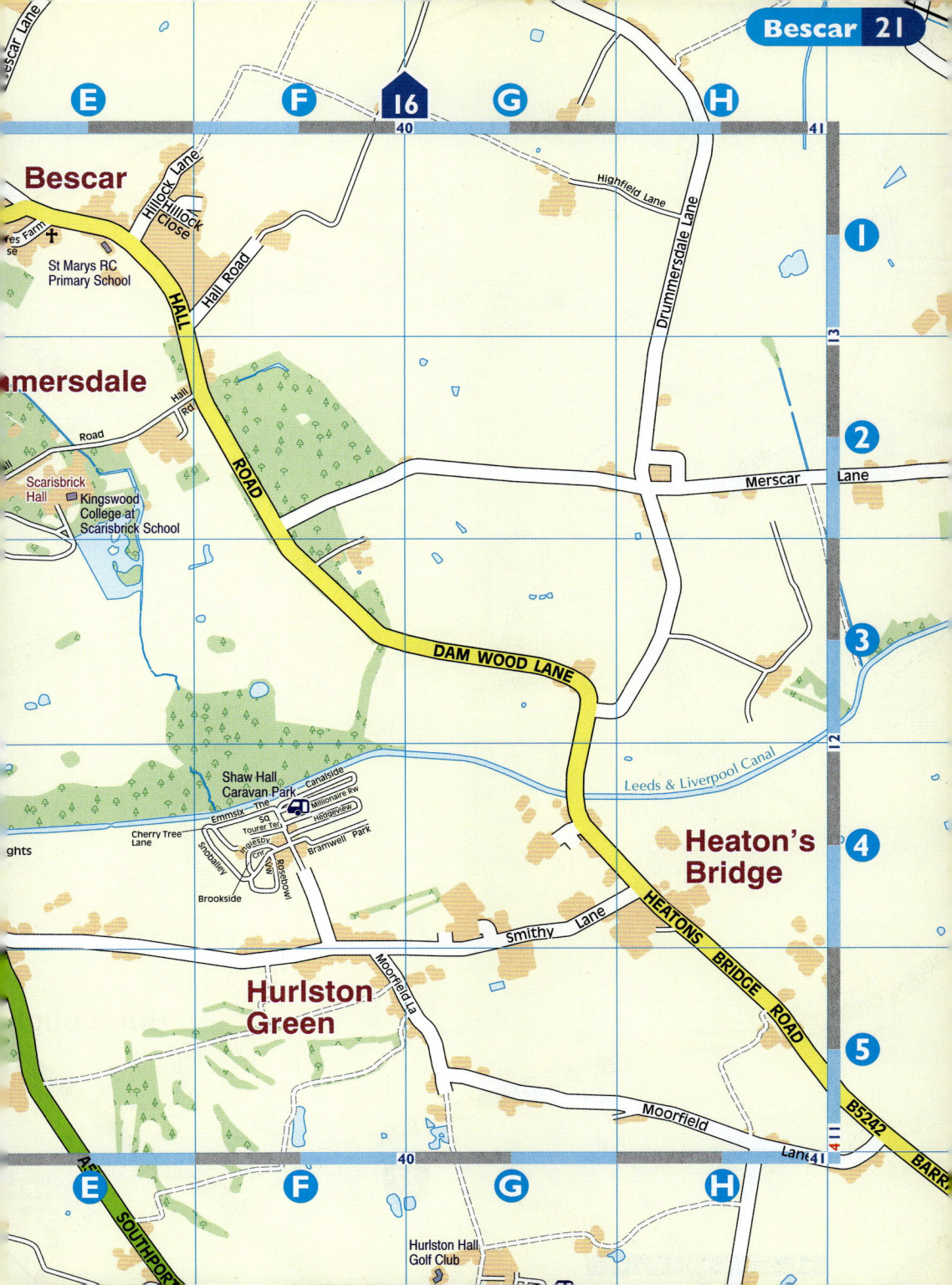

E F **16** 40 G H

I 3

2

Bescar

Hillock Lane
Hillock Close
Highfield Lane

es Farm
se

† St Marys RC
Primary School

HALL

Hall Road

Drummersdale Lane

mersdale

Hall Rd

Road

Scarisbrick
Hall

Kingswood
College at
Scarisbrick School

ROAD

Merscar   Lane

3

DAM WOOD LANE

12

Leeds & Liverpool Canal

Shaw Hall
Caravan Park
Canalside
The
Millionaire Rw
Emmslx
SQ   Hedgeview
Tourer Ter
Cherry Tree   Ingleby
Lane

Snowalley   Bramwell Park

CW
City

Rosebowl

Brookside

ghts

**Heaton's
Bridge**

4

Smithy   Lane

HEATONS

Moorfield La

**Hurlston
Green**

BRIDGE

ROAD

5

Moorfield

B5242

Lane 41

BARR

E F 40 G H 41

SOUTHPOR

Hurlston Hall
Golf Club

22

New Lane

Marsh Moss House

A B C D

New Lane Station

LC

3 42 43

13

1

Gorst Lane Works

New Lane

Crabtree Lane

Martin Hall

12

2

Martin Lane

Burscough Industrial Estate

Langley Place

Langley Road

Gilbert Place

L40

3

Rabbit Lane

Ringtail Road

Plantation Road

Industrial Estate

Higgin's La.

Ringtail Road

Ringtail Court

Ringtail Place

Edge Farm

4

Rabbit Lane

Tollgate Road

Tollgate Crescent

11

Ringtail Industrial Estate

Burscough

BARRISON GREEN

Stub Lane

5

PIPPIN STREET B5242

Guys Industrial Estate

Lordsgate Lane

Surgery

LIVERPOO

A59

Tollgate Road

3 42 43

A B **27** C D

Bluebacre Lane

Merridale Farm

Abbey L. Industrial Estate

Abbey Lane

1 grid square represents 500 metres

E F G H

44 45 13

I

Burscough Bridge

2

New S
House

Moss Lane A59

Back Nook
Cherry Grove
Mere Avenue
Red Cat Lane
Moss Lane

Laburnum Grove

Rowan Cl

Warper's

Moss Lane

Warper's Moss Lane

Burscough Br Station

Burscough Sports Centre

Works

Trent Close

Weaver Avenue

Almond Avenue
Laurel Avenue
Will Cl
Wr M Cl

St Johns CE Primary School

School Lane

LC

Orrell Lane

Burscough FC

Bobby Langton Av
Mart Lane

PO

Burscough Health Cen

Lord Street

Surg

Stanley Court

Burscough Primary Sch

Burscough CC

12

LC

Sutch Lane

Works

Victoria St

Priory Close
School House Gv
Vicarage Gdns

Leeds & Liverpool Canal

Burscough Bridge Methodist Primary School

Liverpool Road North

Mill Lane

Colburne Close

3

Abbey Fold
Vicarage Gardens
Harding Road
Hesketh Road
Pickles Drive
Furnival Drive
Christines Crs
Trevor Road
Truscott Road
Alexandra Road

Burscough Priory Science College

Langdale Drive
Fletchers Dr
Glenroyd Drive
Lathom Close
Mid Av
H Av
Birch Av

Mill Lane

Delph Dr

Hawthorn Av
Green Cl
Boundary La

Broom Cl

Delph Dr

Heather Close

Junction Lane

Burscough Junction Stn

Willow End

Lordsgate Township CE Primary School

Lordsgate Drive

B5241

Gower Gdns

Rees Park

Abbey Dale

Croft Av

Carver Wy

Delph Dr

The Woodlands

4

Liverpool Road South A59

Rivington Drive
Rivington Drive
Blmn Cl

Richmond Avenue

Windsor Cr

Council Building

Ellerbrook Dr

Briars Lane

Leeds & Liverpool Canal

A5209

Meadowbrook

PO

The Poplars

Elm Road

Square Lane A5209

Flaxfields

Brooklands Grove

Flax Lane

Briars Brook

A5209

Three Oaks Close

5

Springfield Close

Platts La

Chapel Lane

St Johns Catholic Primary School

Road South

Manor Avenue
Manor Rd
Manor Crs
Manor Gardens

Platts Lane Industrial Estate

44 45

E F G H

Hall Lane B5240

19

Keswick Close
Bowness Av
Ainsdale Clinic
The Brkdle
Kings Meadow
Primary School
Sandbrook Road
Kings Meadow
Meadow Lane
Lane
E
F
Meadow Lan
32
G
H
33
Dorset Dr
Sorset Dr
Avenue Way
A565
LIVERPOOL ROAD
Rose Crs
Cherry Road
Heather Cl
Lilac Av
St John Stone
Catholic Primary
School
Dunlop Avenue
Woodvale Road
Vale Crescent
Moor
Close
Woodvale
Road
I
Moor Lane
Liverpool Old Road
Plex Moss Lane
Lancashire County
Sefton
Plex Moss Lane
2
Gettern Farm
10
Golf Course
3
Broad Lane
Formby Hall
Golf &
Country Club
Alder
Lane
4
North Moss Lane
409
5
Sefton
Lancashire County
32
Cheshire Lines Path
33
E
F
G
H
Moss Lane
Downholland Brook

ORMSKIRK

1 grid square represents 500 metres

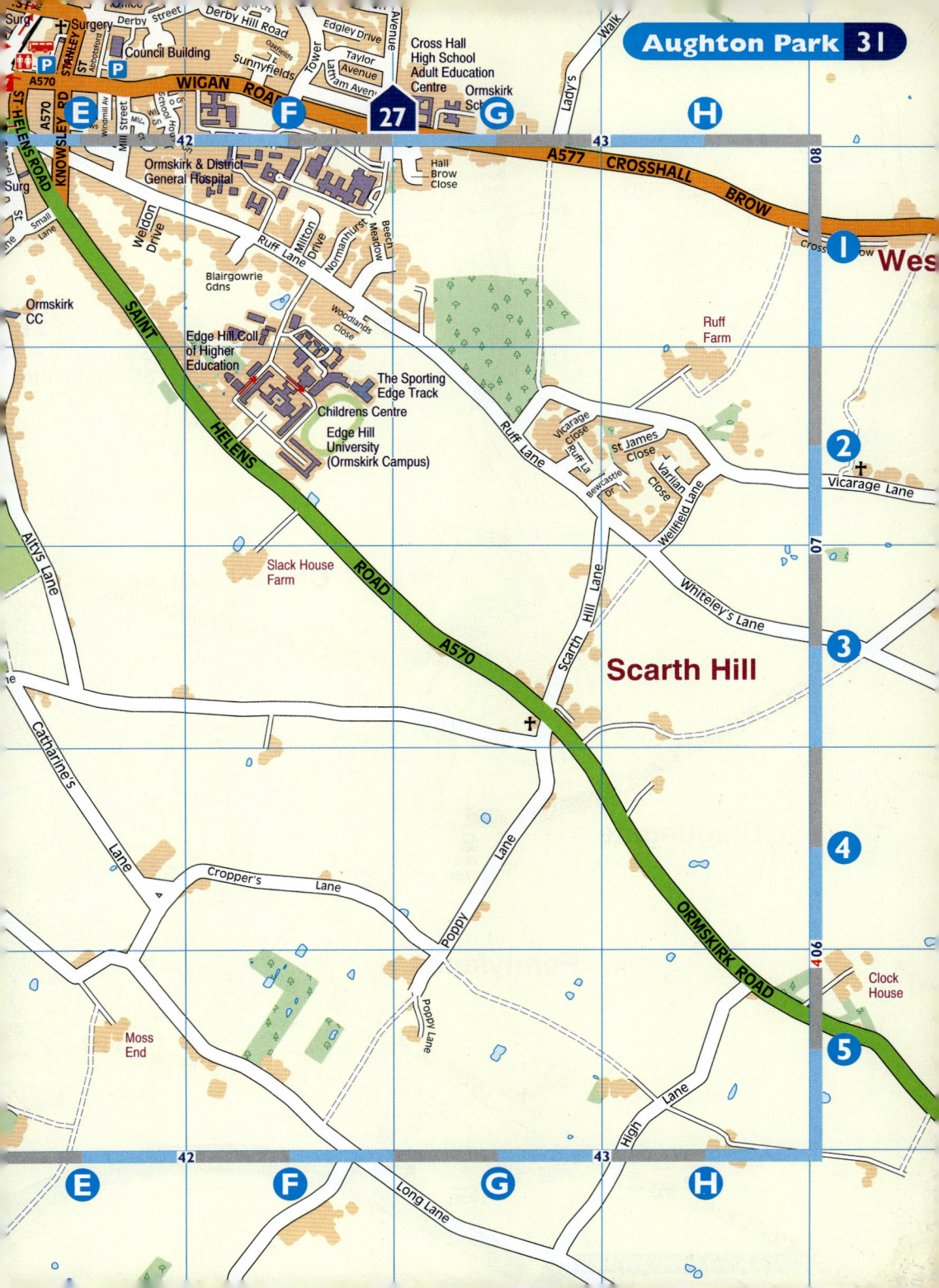

Surg

St

Surgery

Council Building

Derby Street

Derby Hill Road

Edgley Drive

Avenue

Cross Hall High School Adult Education Centre

Ormskirk Sch

WIGAN ROAD

Oakfields

Tower

Taylor Avenue

Latham Avenue

Sunnyfields

STANLEY ST

St Abbotsford

Mill Street

Windmill Av

School Lane

Mill

St Cr

ST HELENS RD

KNOWSLEY RD

A570

A570

P

P

E

F

G

H

27

Ormskirk & District General Hospital

Hall Brow Close

42

43

08

A577 CROSSHALL BROW

Cross Hall Brow

Wes

I

Weldon Drive

Ruff Lane

Milton Drive

Normanhurst

Beech Meadow

Blairgowrie Gdns

Woodlands Close

Ruff Farm

Ormskirk CC

Edge Hill Coll of Higher Education

SAINT HELENS ROAD

A570

The Sporting Edge Track

Childrens Centre

Edge Hill University (Ormskirk Campus)

Ruff Lane

Vicarage Close

Ruff Ln

St James Close

Bewcastle Dr

Varlian Close

Wellfield Lane

Vicarage Lane

2

Altys Lane

Slack House Farm

Scarth Hill Lane

Whiteley's Lane

07

3

Catharine's Lane

Scarth Hill

†

Cropper's Lane

Poppy Lane

ORMSKIRK ROAD

4

406

Clock House

5

Moss End

Poppy Lane

High Lane

Long Lane

E

F

G

H

42

43

Cobb's Lane Clough

E

Whalleys Road

W Valley 33

F

Newton Dr

Needham

Newby

Lane

G

Beech

H

Michael
CE Primary Schoo

CE Primary School

I

Briars Green

St James
RC Primary
School

Kestrel
Mews

Middlewood

Ashmead

Maplewood

Rowan

Maytree Walk

Meadow

Kestral Park

Merewood

Ashurst Gdns

Hazel

Northfield

Melbreck

Mountwood

Maplewood

Ashurst Road

Ashurst
Health Centre

Kingsbury
Ct

Pinewood

2

Beechwood

Summer

Street

Ashmead

Road

Manfield

Larkhill

Lambourne

Lindens

Lulworth

Ashby

Forest drive

Our Lady
een of Peace
tholic High School

Ashurst PO

Ashurst

Foxfold

Lathom
High School

Cobbs Brow
Comm School

Ashurst Rd

Ashley

Ledburn

Low Croft

Elm

HOUGHTONS ROAD A577

El
Gr

A577 HOUGHTONS ROAD

Irwell

Fawcett

Fairburn

Fair haven

Fairlie CP
School

Fairstead

Falkland

Birch green Road

Inskip

Birch Green Road

Ivybridge

Feltons

Felstead

Heversham

Helmsdale

Tawd Valley
Park

Inglewhite

Ivydale

Ferndale

Woodland
Primary
School

Hallcroft

Harsnips

Hartshead

Parklands

3

34

Crow Orchard
Primary
School

SKELMERSDALE

Superstore PO

Inchfield

Northway

Birch Green

Birch Green

Findon

Firbeck

Flamstead

Flaxton

Flordon

St Edmunds
Catholic
Primary
School

Yewdale

Skelmersdale &
Ormskirk Colleges
(Northway Centre)

Nye Bevan
Swimming
Pool

Police
Station

Market Hall
Concourse
Shop Cen

Northway

St Johns
RC Primary
School

Hillside
Health
Centre

4

Yeadon

Southway

GLENBURN ROAD

Willow Hey

Windrows

Windrows

Glenburn
Sports Coll

Skelmersdale
& Ormskirk Colleges
(Westbank Centre)

Eskdale

Delph Side
Primary
School

Eskbank

Eskbank

Tanhous

Elswick

Elmstead

Tanhouse

5

HOPE
ISLAND

Winstanley
Road

GRIMSHAW ROAD

Southway

GRIMSHAW

Hillside
Community
Primary Sch

Greenev
Place

Works

Gratton
Place

Glebe Road

Postal
Delivery
Office

Whiteledge
Centre

Ormskirk

Road

GRIMSHAW

ROAD

B5312

Fir Tree
Road

Junction 4

E

A5068

Gillibrands Road

F

Grimrod Place

Corsey

G

Top Acre

Ske
Sports
Centre

H

Fire
Station

St Francis of
Assisi Catholic
Primary School

East
Gillbrands
Industrial

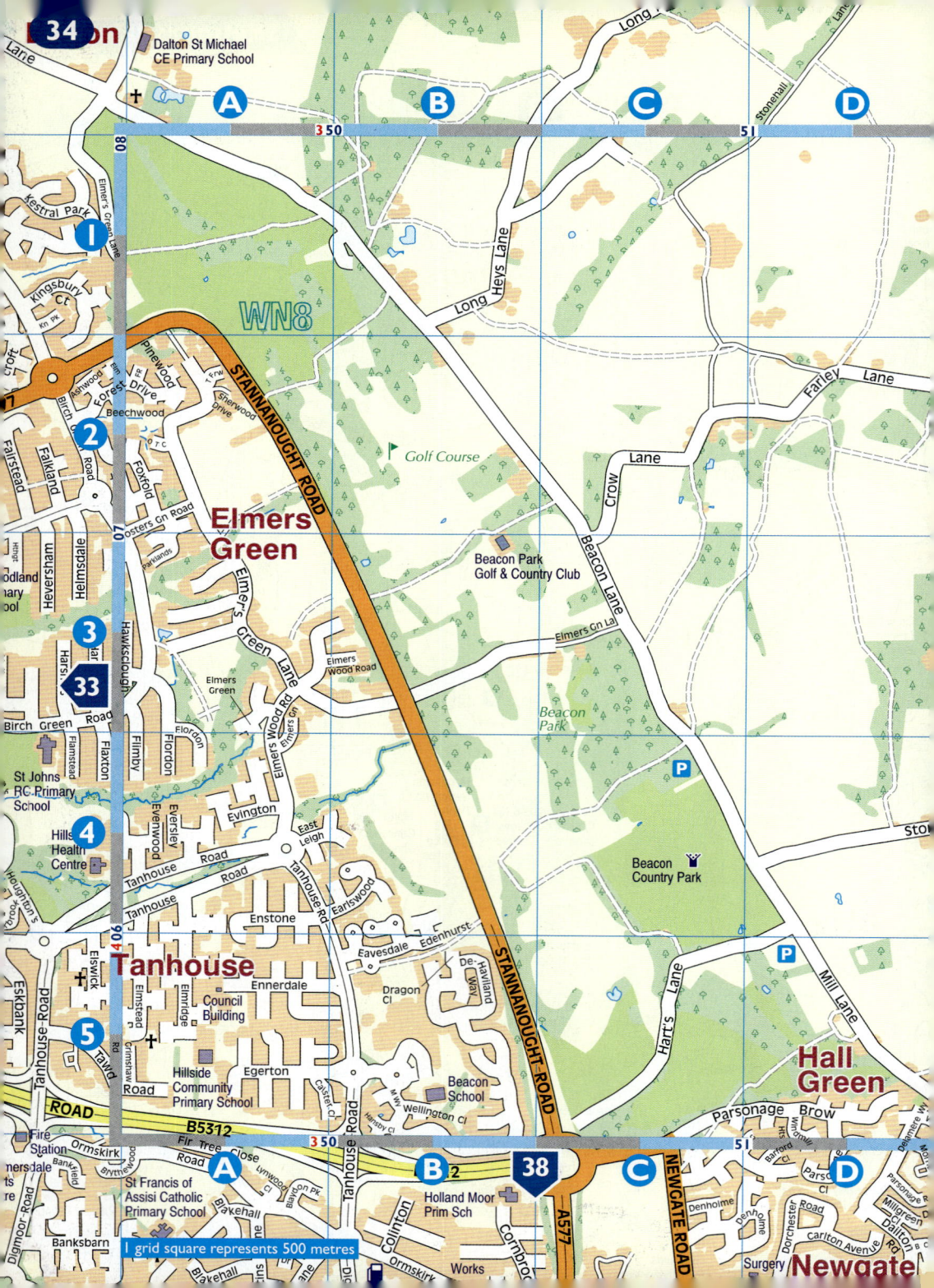

on

Dalton St Michael
CE Primary School

A   **3** 50   **B**   **C**   51   **D**

I

Kestral Park
Elmer's Green Lane
Kingsbury Ct
Kn Pk
Croft

WN8

Long Heys Lane

Long

Farley Lane

2
Ashwood
Forest Drive
Birch Rd
Pinewood
Beechwood
Sherwood Drive
D T C

STANNANOUGHT ROAD

Golf Course

Crow Lane

Beacon Lane

Fairstead
Falkland
Heversham
Helmsdale
Woodland
mary
ool

Oosters Gn Road
Parklands

**Elmers
Green**

Elmer's Green Lane

Beacon Park
Golf & Country Club

Elmers Gn La

3
Har's
Hawksclough
Elmers
Green

33

Elmers
Wood Road

Elmers Wood Rd
Elmers Gn

Beacon
Park

Birch Green Road
Flamsted
Flaxton
Flimby
Flaxton
Florton
Florton

P

St Johns
RC Primary
School

Eversley
Evington
East
Leigh

Beacon
Country Park

4
Hills
Health
Centre

Evenwood
Tanhouse Road
Tanhouse Rd
Earlswood

P

Houghton's

Tanhouse Road
Enstone

Tanhouse
Elswick
Elmstead
Elmridge
Council
Building
Ennerdale
Eavesdale
Edenhurst
De-Way
Haviland
Dragon
Cl

STANNANOUGHT ROAD

Hart's Lane

Mill Lane

Sto

**Hall
Green**

5
Eskbank
Tawd
Hillside
Community
Primary School
Egerton
Caister Cl
M.W.
Hansby Cl
Wellington Cl
Beacon
School

Parsonage Brow
Debarne W
Barford
Cl
Pars
Cl
Denholme

ROAD
B5312   **3** 50   51

NEWGATE ROAD

Dorchester Road
Carlton Avenue
Denholme
denholm
Dalton
Millgreen
Parsonage

A   **B** 2   **38**   **C**   **D**

Fire
Station
Ormskirk
Bank
St Francis of
Assisi Catholic
Primary School
Blakehall
Colinton
Holland Moor
Prim Sch
Cornbro
A577
Surgery
Newgate
Banksbarn
Blakehall
Ormskirk
Works

Digmoor Road
ts
rt

Fir Tree Close
Lynwood
Cl
Brandon

Carlton Avenue

I grid square represents 500 metres

Holland Lees

Farm

Golf Course

E 52 F Bank Road G 53 H 08 I

Brow

Bank Top

Ba...

Leeds & Liverpool Canal

Ayrefield Road

Gabriel Cl

Whitley Road

Roby Mill CE Primary School

Cemetery

School Lane

Roby Mill

Stoney Brow

Lafford Lane

2 Gath

M6 07

Dean Wood

3

Whitley Road

Whitley Rd

St Teresas Catholic Primary School

Gathurst Road

4

GATHURST

Dean Wood Av

A406

Spring Road

Eton Av

Way

Cambridge Road

Derwent Road

College Road

Golf Course

5

Coniston Avenue

Oxford Rd

Oldfield Road

Lafford Lane

Dean Wood Golf Club

Dingle Av

Woodside Cl

Grs Av

Windermere Rd

Thrimere Rd

GROVE ROAD

Hillside

Rydal Av

Ullswater Av

Thames Av

Win Clo

Millers Nook

HallBridge Gardens

Grasmere Av

PARLIAMENT STREET

DINGLE ROAD

E 52 F 39 G 53 H

St Thomas The Martyr CE Prim.Sch

Surgery

Bridgehall Cl

PO

Hall Green

Alma Hill

Rivington Dr

Priory Rd

Abbey Cl

Priory Nook

Brooklands

Mill House Vw

Spencer's Lane

Orrell Post

Douglas

St Peters Catholic School

Works

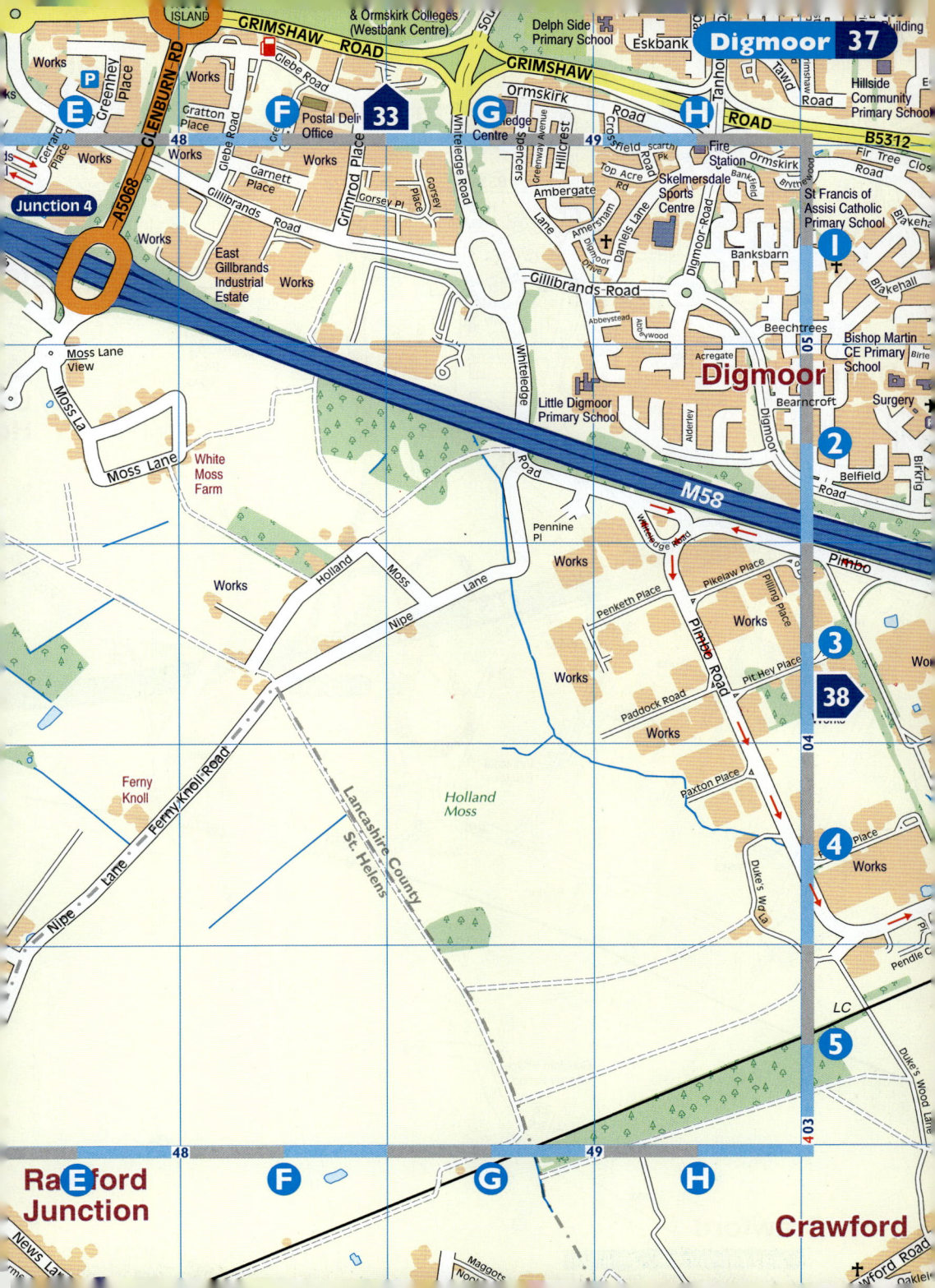

Ainsdale	E3 19	Carr Cross	F5 15	Higher End	F5 39	Roby Mill	E2
Ainsdale-on-Sea	A3 18	Carr Houses	G3 41	High Park	B2 10	Scarisbrick	C1
Ashurst	G1 33	Chapel House	C3 32	Hillside	B3 12	Scarth Hill	H3
Aughton Park	D3 30	Churchtown	D1 10	Hurlston Green	F5 21	Skelmersdale	F3
Banks	D1 6	Crossens	H3 5	Ince Blundell	F4 41	Snape Green	G4
Bank Top	F1 35	Digmoor	H2 37	Lady Green	F3 41	Southport	C1
Bescar	E1 21	Drummersdale	D2 20	Little Altcar	G5 29	Stanley	D2
Birch Green	H3 33	Elmers Green	A2 34	Marshside	E4 5	Tanhouse	H5
Birkdale	D3 12	Far Moor	H3 39	Newgate	D1 38	Tontine	G2
Blaguegate	A4 32	Fiddler's Ferry	B1 6	Ormskirk	B5 26	Up Holland	D2
Blowick	A4 10	Formby	E2 29	Orrell Post	H1 39	Woodvale	D5
Brown Edge	C3 14	Freshfield	C1 28	Pennylands	B5 32	
Burscough	D5 22	Hall Green	D5 34	Pinfold	D4 20	
Burscough Bridge	E1 23	Heaton's Bridge	H4 21	Pool Hey	D2 14	

USING THE STREET INDEX

Street names are listed alphabetically. Each street name is followed by its postal town or area locality, the Postcode District, the page number, and the reference to the square in which the name is found.

Standard index entries are shown as follows:

Abbey Cl *FMBY* L37 ....**25** E2

Street names and selected addresses not shown on the map due to scale restrictions are shown in the index with an asterisk:

Admiralty Cl *BRSC* L40 * **22** D5

GENERAL ABBREVIATIONS

ACC	ACCESS	EMB	EMBANKMENT	LK	LOCK
ALY	ALLEY	EMBY	EMBASSY	LKS	LAKES
AP	APPROACH	ESP	ESPLANADE	LNDG	LANDING
AR	ARCADE	EST	ESTATE	LTL	LITTLE
ASS	ASSOCIATION	EX	EXCHANGE	LWR	LOWER
AV	AVENUE	EXPY	EXPRESSWAY	MAG	MAGISTRATES'
BCH	BEACH	EXT	EXTENSION	MAN	MANSIONS
BLDS	BUILDINGS	F/O	FLYOVER	MD	MEAD
BND	BEND	FC	FOOTBALL CLUB	MDW	MEADOWS
BNK	BANK	FK	FORK	MEM	MEMORIAL
BR	BRIDGE	FLD	FIELD	MI	MILL
BRK	BROOK	FLDS	FIELDS	MKT	MARKET
BTM	BOTTOM	FLS	FALLS	MKTS	MARKETS
BUS	BUSINESS	FM	FARM	ML	MALL
BVD	BOULEVARD	FT	FORT	MNR	MANOR
BY	BYPASS	FTS	FLATS	MS	MEWS
CATH	CATHEDRAL	FWY	FREEWAY	MSN	MISSION
CEM	CEMETERY	FY	FERRY	MT	MOUNT
CEN	CENTRE	GA	GATE	MTN	MOUNTAIN
CFT	CROFT	GAL	GALLERY	MTS	MOUNTAINS
CH	CHURCH	GDN	GARDEN	MUS	MUSEUM
CHA	CHASE	GDNS	GARDENS	MWY	MOTORWAY
CHYD	CHURCHYARD	GLD	GLADE	N	NORTH
CIR	CIRCLE	GLN	GLEN	NE	NORTH EAST
CIRC	CIRCUS	GN	GREEN	NW	NORTH WEST
CL	CLOSE	GND	GROUND	O/P	OVERPASS
CLFS	CLIFFS	GRA	GRANGE	OFF	OFFICE
CMP	CAMP	GRG	GARAGE	ORCH	ORCHARD
CNR	CORNER	GT	GREAT	OV	OVAL
CO	COUNTY	GTWY	GATEWAY	PAL	PALACE
COLL	COLLEGE	GV	GROVE	PAS	PASSAGE
COM	COMMON	HGR	HIGHER	PAV	PAVILION
COMM	COMMISSION	HL	HILL	PDE	PARADE
CON	CONVENT	HLS	HILLS	PH	PUBLIC HOUSE
COT	COTTAGE	HO	HOUSE	PK	PARK
COTS	COTTAGES	HOL	HOLLOW	PKWY	PARKWAY
CP	CAPE	HOSP	HOSPITAL	PL	PLACE
CPS	COPSE	HRB	HARBOUR	PLN	PLAIN
CR	CREEK	HTH	HEATH	PLNS	PLAINS
CREM	CREMATORIUM	HTS	HEIGHTS	PLZ	PLAZA
CRS	CRESCENT	HVN	HAVEN	POL	POLICE STATION
CSWY	CAUSEWAY	HWY	HIGHWAY	PR	PRINCE
CT	COURT	IMP	IMPERIAL	PREC	PRECINCT
CTRL	CENTRAL	IN	INLET	PREP	PREPARATORY
CTS	COURTS	IND EST	INDUSTRIAL ESTATE	PRIM	PRIMARY
CTYD	COURTYARD	INF	INFIRMARY	PROM	PROMENADE
CUTT	CUTTINGS	INFO	INFORMATION	PRS	PRINCESS
CV	COVE	INT	INTERCHANGE	PRT	PORT
CYN	CANYON	IS	ISLAND	PT	POINT
DEPT	DEPARTMENT	JCT	JUNCTION	PTH	PATH
DL	DALE	JTY	JETTY	PZ	PIAZZA
DM	DAM	KG	KING	QD	QUADRANT
DR	DRIVE	KNL	KNOLL	QU	QUEEN
DRO	DROVE	L	LAKE	QY	QUAY
DRY	DRIVEWAY	LA	LANE	R	RIVER
DWGS	DWELLINGS	LDG	LODGE	RBT	ROUNDABOUT
E	EAST	LGT	LIGHT	RD	ROAD

RDG	RIDG
REP	REPUBLI
RES	RESERVOI
RFC	RUGBY FOOTBALL CLU
RI	RIS
RP	RAM
RW	ROV
S	SOUT
SCH	SCHOO
SE	SOUTH EAS
SER	SERVICE ARE
SH	SHOR
SHOP	SHOPPIN
SKWY	SKYWA
SMT	SUMMI
SOC	SOCIET
SP	SPU
SPR	SPRIN
SQ	SQUAR
ST	STREE
STN	STATIO
STR	STREAM
STRD	STRAN
SW	SOUTH WES
TDG	TRADIN
TER	TERRAC
THWY	THROUGHWA
TNL	TUNNE
TOLL	TOLLWA
TPK	TURNPIK
TR	TRAC
TRL	TRAI
TWR	TCWE
U/P	UNDERPAS
UNI	UNIVERSIT
UPR	UPPE
V	VAL
VA	VALLE
VIAD	VIADUC
VIL	VILL
VIS	VIST
VLG	VILLAG
VLS	VILLA
VW	VIEW
W	WES
WD	WOO
WHF	WHAR
WK	WAL
WKS	WALK
WLS	WELL
WY	WA
YD	YAR
YHA	YOUTH HOSTE

POSTCODE TOWNS AND AREA ABBREVIATIONS

BRSC	Burscough	HTWN	Hightown	RNFD/HAY	Rainford/Haydock	WGNNW/ST	Wigan northwest
CHTN/BK	Churchtown/Banks	KIRK/FR/WAR	Kirkham/	SFTN	Sefton		Standis
CSBY/BLUN	Crosby/Blundellsands		Freckleton/Warton	SKEL	Skelmersdale	WGNW/BIL/OR	Wigan west
FMBY	Formby	ORM	Ormskirk	STHP	Southport		Billinge/Crre

A

bey Cl *FMBY* L37 ....29 H4
SKEL WN8 ....39 F1
bbey Dl *BRSC* L40 ....23 C4
bbey Dr *WGNW/BIL/OR* WN5 ...39 H2
bbey Fold *BRSC* L40 ....23 E2
bbey Gdns *STHP* PR8 ....13 E1
bbey La *CHTN/BK* PR9 ....3 G1
bbey Ter *STHP* PR8 ....9 E5
bbeystead *SKEL* WN8 ....37 C1
bbeywood *SKEL* WN8 ....37 H1
bbots Cl *FMBY* L37 ....29 G5
bbotsford *ORM* L39 ....27 E5
bbots Wy *FMBY* L37 ....29 G4
bington Dr *STHP* PR8 ....7 E2
brams Fold *CHTN/BK* PR9 ....6 D2
brams Gn *CHTN/BK* PR9 ....6 D2
e Acorns *ORM* L39 ....30 D2
cregate *SKEL* WN8 ....37 H2
dmiralty Cl *BRSC* L40 * 22 D5
ntree Cres *STHP* PR8 ....14 B2
bert Pl *CHTN/BK* PR9 ....9 F1
bert Rd *CHTN/BK* PR9 ....3 G2
bert Ter *STHP* PR8 ....9 E5
berdale Av *STHP* PR8 ....18 C3
der La *FMBY* L37 ....25 G3
derley Rd *SKEL* WN8 ....37 H2
derson Crs *FMBY* L37 ....29 F2
exander Cl *BRSC* L40 ....23 E3
exandra Cl *SKEL* WN8 ....32 D5
exandra Ms *CHTN/BK* PR9 ....3 K1
ORM L39 ....26 D4
exandra Rd *BRSC* L40 ....23 E3
CHTN/BK PR9 ....3 K1
lerton Rd *CHTN/BK* PR9 ....10 A1
ma Cl *SKEL* WN8 ....39 F1
ma Ct *SKEL* WN8 ....39 F1
ma Hl *SKEL* WN8 ....39 F1
ma Rd *SKEL* WN8 ....39 F1
STHP PR8 ....13 E1
mond Av *BRSC* L40 ....23 F5
tcar La *FMBY* L37 ....29 F5
tcar Rd *FMBY* L37 ....29 G4
cham Rd *STHP* PR8 ....14 A3
thorpe Dr *STHP* PR8 ....7 H2
ton Cl *HTWN* L38 ....40 A5
t Rd *FMBY* L37 ....29 F5
HTWN L38 ....40 A3
tys La *ORM* L39 ....31 E2
nbergate *SKEL* WN8 ....37 G1
nersham *SKEL* WN8 ....37 H1
chor St *CHTN/BK* PR9 ....3 H3
dreas Cl *FMBY* L37 ....13 F1
drews Cl *FMBY* L37 ....29 E5
drews La *FMBY* L37 ....29 E5
drews Yort *FMBY* L37 ....29 E5
nandale Gdns *SKEL* WN8 ....38 D1
ne Av *STHP* PR8 ....19 G2
n St *SKEL* WN8 ....32 D4
sdell Cl *CHTN/BK* PR9 ....5 G3
avil Cl *WGNW/BIL/OR* WN5 ....39 G4
pleton Rd *SKEL* WN8 ....33 E3
bour St *STHP* PR8 ....3 J6
den Cl *STHP* PR8 ....18 C2
dleigh Av *STHP* PR8 ....14 A2
rgameols Cl *STHP* PR8 ....10 B5
rgarmeols Gv *FMBY* L37 ....24 A5
rgarmeols Rd *FMBY* L37 ....24 A5
rgyle Rd *CHTN/BK* PR9 ....9 H1
lington Cl *STHP* PR8 ....18 C3
nside Rd *CHTN/BK* PR9 ....3 J3
nside Ter *CHTN/BK* PR9 ....3 K3
undel Rd *STHP* PR8 ....12 D5
cot Cl *STHP* PR8 ....8 C5
h Cl *ORM* L39 ....26 C5
hcroft Av *ORM* L39 ....27 E4
hcroft Rd *FMBY* L37 ....29 G4
hdale La *FMBY* L37 ....28 C3
hdown Cl *STHP* PR8 ....13 H1
h Gv *FMBY* L37 ....28 C5
SKEL WN8 ....32 C4
hley Rd *CHTN/BK* PR9 ....5 G3
h La *SKEL* WN8 ....33 G2
hmead Rd *SKEL* WN8 ....33 F1
h St *STHP* PR8 ....1 K7
hton Rd *STHP* PR8 ....12 D4
hurst Cl *SKEL* WN8 ....33 F1
hurst St *FMBY* L37 ....29 E4
hurst Gdns *SKEL* WN8 ....33 F1
hwall St *SKEL* WN8 ....33 H2
hwood *SKEL* WN8 ....33 H2
land Gdns *CHTN/BK* PR9 ....6 A3
mall Cl *ORM* L39 ....26 B4
mall La *ORM* L39 ....26 B4
pen Gv *FMBY* L37 ....28 C5
nole Gv *CHTN/BK* PR9 ....10 B3

Aughton Park Dr *ORM* L39 ....30 C3
Aughton Rd *STHP* PR8 ....2 E7
Aughton St *ORM* L39 ....30 C1
Aveling Dr *CHTN/BK* PR9 ....7 E1
Avenham Cl *CHTN/BK* PR9 ....7 F2
The Avenue *CHTN/BK* PR9 ....6 D2
CHTN/BK PR9 ....11 H5
ORM L39 ....26 C4
WGNW/BIL/OR WN5 ....39 G5
Avondale Rd *CHTN/BK* PR9 ....3 H1
Avondale Rd North *CHTN/BK* PR9 ..9 G1
Ayr Cl *STHP* PR8 ....14 B1
Ayrefield Rd *SKEL* WN8 ....35 F1

B

Back Bath St *CHTN/BK* PR9 ....3 G2
Back Forest Rd *STHP* PR8 ....9 H4
Back La *BRSC* L40 ....27 H5
SKEL WN8 ....38 A2
Back O The Town La *HTWN* L38 .....41 F4
Back Rw *SKEL* WN8 ....38 A2
Back School La *SKEL* WN8 ....32 C4
SKEL WN8 ....39 F1
Back Virginia St *STHP* PR8 ....3 H6
Badgers Rake *FMBY* L37 ....28 C1
Baker's La *CHTN/BK* PR9 ....5 F4
Balfour Rd *STHP* PR8 ....10 A5
Balmoral Cl *CHTN/BK* PR9 ....5 H4
Balmoral Dr *CHTN/BK* PR9 ....5 H4
FMBY L37 ....29 E5
Bamber Gdns *CHTN/BK* PR9 ....10 C2
Banastre Rd *STHP* PR8 ....9 E5
Bank Av *WGNW/BIL/OR* WN5 ....39 H3
Bank Brow *SKEL* WN8 ....35 F1
Bankfield *SKEL* WN8 ....37 H1
Bankfield La *CHTN/BK* PR9 ....5 H5
Bank Nook *CHTN/BK* PR9 * 5 H5
Banksbarn *SKEL* WN8 ....37 H1
Bankside *HTWN* L38 ....40 A4
Bank Sq *SKEL* WN8 ....3 G1
Banks Rd *CHTN/BK* PR9 ....6 B1
Bardsley Cl *SKEL* WN8 ....38 D1
Barford Cl *SKEL* WN8 ....38 D1
STHP PR8 ....18 C2
Barkfield Cl *FMBY* L37 ....28 D2
Barkfield La *FMBY* L37 ....28 D2
Barnes Rd *ORM* L39 ....30 D2
SKEL WN8 ....32 C4
Barnfield Dr *SKEL* WN8 ....38 D1
Barrett Av *STHP* PR8 ....13 E3
Barrett Rd *STHP* PR8 ....13 E3
Barrington Dr *STHP* PR8 ....18 D3
Barton Heys Rd *FMBY* L37 ....28 D5
Bartons Cl *STHP* PR8 ....9 B2
Bath Springs *ORM* L39 ....27 E5
Bath St *CHTN/BK* PR9 ....3 G2
Bath St North *CHTN/BK* PR9 ....3 G2
Battle Wy *FMBY* L37 * 29 H4
Baytree Cl *STHP* PR8 ....10 A3
Beacham Rd *STHP* PR8 ....10 A3
Beach Priory Gdns *STHP* PR8 ....2 D5
Beach Rd *STHP* PR8 ....2 C6
Beacon La *SKEL* WN8 ....34 C3
Beaconsfield Rd *CHTN/BK* PR9 .....10 B4
Beacon View Dr *SKEL* WN8 ....39 E1
Bearncroft *SKEL* WN8 ....37 H2
Beatty Rd *STHP* PR8 ....10 A5
Beaufort *FMBY* L37 ....29 G4
Beaumont Crs *ORM* L39 ....30 C3
Beavers La *SKEL* WN8 ....38 A1
Bebles Rd *ORM* L39 ....30 B2
Bedford Rd *STHP* PR8 ....13 E3
Beech Cl *SKEL* WN8 ....32 D4
Beech Dr *FMBY* L37 ....29 H2
Beechfield Gdns *STHP* PR8 ....2 D5
Beech Gv *CHTN/BK* PR9 ....5 H5
Beech Meadow *ORM* L39 ....31 F1
Beechtrees *SKEL* WN8 ....37 H1
Beechwood *SKEL* WN8 ....33 H1
Beechwood Crs
WGNW/BIL/OR WN5 ....39 H2
Beechwood Dr *FMBY* L37 ....28 C5
ORM L39 ....30 C1
Beeford Dr *WGNW/BIL/OR* WN5 ..39 H3
Belfield *SKEL* WN8 ....38 A2
Belgrave Rd *STHP* PR8 ....9 H4
Bellis Av *CHTN/BK* PR9 ....5 E5
Belmont Av *WGNW/BIL/OR* WN5 ..39 G5
Belmont Cl *BRSC* L40 ....23 F4
Belmont St *STHP* PR8 ....2 E6
Belvedere Dr *FMBY* L37 ....29 F5
Belvedere Rd *CHTN/BK* PR9 ....19 E3
Bengarth Rd *CHTN/BK* PR9 ....10 B2
Bennett Dr *WGNW/BIL/OR* WN5 ..39 G4
Bentham St *STHP* PR8 ....3 G7
Bentham's Wy *STHP* PR8 ....13 G4

Beresford Dr *CHTN/BK* PR9 ....10 B1
Beresford Gdns *CHTN/BK* PR9 ....5 F5
Berry Cl *SKEL* WN8 ....33 E3
Berry House Rd *BRSC* L40 ....17 G1
Berry St *SKEL* WN8 ....32 D5
Berwick Av *STHP* PR8 ....19 E2
Bescar Brow La *BRSC* L40 ....20 C1
Bescar La *BRSC* L40 ....16 A5
Beverley Cl *CHTN/BK* PR9 ....6 A2
Bewcastle Dr *BRSC* L40 ....31 G2
Bibby Rd *CHTN/BK* PR9 ....10 C1
Bickerton Rd *STHP* PR8 ....12 D1
Birch Av *BRSC* L40 ....23 F3
The Birches *FMBY* L37 ....29 E1
Birch Cl *CHTN/BK* PR9 ....28 D1
Birch Green Rd *SKEL* WN8 ....33 G2
Birch St *SKEL* WN8 ....32 D4
STHP PR8 ....13 F2
Birkdale Cop *STHP* PR8 ....14 A4
Birkey La *STHP* PR8 ....29 F4
Birkrig *SKEL* WN8 ....38 A2
Birleywood *SKEL* WN8 ....38 A2
Bispham Rd *CHTN/BK* PR9 ....10 B3
Blackacre La *BRSC* L40 ....27 E3
Blackcar La *SFTN* L29 ....41 H4
Blackledge Cl
WGNW/BIL/OR WN5 ....39 H3
Black Moss La *BRSC* L40 ....20 B1
ORM L39 ....30 C3
Blaguegate La *SKEL* WN8 ....32 A3
Blairgowrie Gdns *ORM* L39 ....31 F1
Blair Gv *STHP* PR8 ....10 B3
Blakehall *SKEL* WN8 ....38 A1
Blandford Cl *STHP* PR8 ....2 B7
Blaydon Pk *SKEL* WN8 ....38 A1
Blenheim Rd *STHP* PR8 ....18 D2
Blindman's La *ORM* L39 ....26 B3
Blundell Av *FMBY* L37 ....28 B2
HTWN L38 ....40 A4
STHP PR8 ....12 D3
Blundell Crs *STHP* PR8 ....12 D3
Blundell Dr *STHP* PR8 ....12 D3
Blundell Gv *HTWN* L38 ....40 A4
Blundell La *CHTN/BK* PR9 ....4 A5
Blundell Rd *HTWN* L38 ....40 A5
Blythe Ms *STHP* PR8 ....12 D5
Blythewood *SKEL* WN8 ....37 H1
Bobbiners La *CHTN/BK* PR9 ....7 E4
Bobby Langton Wy *BRSC* L40 ....23 F2
Bodmin *CHTN/BK* PR9 ....5 F2
Bold St *CHTN/BK* PR9 ....3 G2
Bolton Cl *STHP* PR8 ....29 G4
Bolton Rd *STHP* PR8 ....13 E1
Bolton's Cop *CHTN/BK* PR9 ....7 H1
Booth St *CHTN/BK* PR9 ....3 G1
Borrowdale Rd *FMBY* L37 ....29 F1
Bosworth Dr *STHP* PR8 ....18 D4
Botanic Rd *CHTN/BK* PR9 ....5 H5
CHTN/BK PR9 ....5 H5
Boundary La *BRSC* L40 ....23 G4
CHTN/BK PR9 ....7 H2
Boundary St *STHP* PR8 ....13 F1
Bowling Green Cl *STHP* PR8 ....10 B5
Bowness Av *STHP* PR8 ....19 E5
Bracebridge Dr *STHP* PR8 ....14 B3
Brackenway *FMBY* L37 ....24 C5
Brade St *CHTN/BK* PR9 ....6 A3
Bradley St *CHTN/BK* PR9 ....3 K2
Bradshaw's La *STHP* PR8 ....19 F2
Braemar Dr *CHTN/BK* PR9 ....5 F2
Bramble Wy *BRSC* L40 ....23 G3
Bramhall Rd *SKEL* WN8 ....33 E3
Bramwell Pk *BRSC* L40 ....21 F4
Brandon Cl *SKEL* WN8 ....38 D1
Breeze Rd *STHP* PR8 ....12 C3
Brentwood Cl *HTWN* L38 ....40 A5
Brentwood Ct *STHP* PR8 ....14 B3
Bretton Fold *STHP* PR8 ....10 B5
Brewery La *FMBY* L37 ....24 B5
Briar Rd *STHP* PR8 ....19 F4
Briars Brook *BRSC* L40 ....23 H4
Briars Gn *SKEL* WN8 ....33 F1
Briars La *BRSC* L40 ....23 H4
The Briars *STHP* PR8 ....12 D4
Briary Cft *HTWN* L38 ....40 A4
Bridge Av *ORM* L39 ....30 D1
Bridge Gv *STHP* PR8 ....3 H6
Bridgehall Dr *SKEL* WN8 ....39 E1
Bridgend Dr *STHP* PR8 ....18 D4
Bridge St *ORM* L39 ....30 D1
STHP PR8 ....29 H4
Bridge Wills La *CHTN/BK* PR9 ....6 A2
Brierfield *SKEL* WN8 ....38 A3
Brighouse Cl *ORM* L39 ....26 C4
Brighton Rd *STHP* PR8 ....19 F2
Brightstone Cl *CHTN/BK* PR9 ....7 E2
Bright St *CHTN/BK* PR9 ....10 B3
Brinklow Cl *STHP* PR8 ....18 C3
Broadacre *SKEL* WN8 ....38 D2

Broadlands *STHP* PR8 ....12 C2
Broad La *FMBY* L37 ....24 D4
Broadway Cl *STHP* PR8 ....18 D3
Brocklebank Rd *CHTN/BK* PR9 .....10 A1
Bromilow Rd *SKEL* WN8 ....32 B4
Brompton Rd *STHP* PR8 ....10 A3
The Brookdale *STHP* PR8 ....19 F5
Brooke Cl *CHTN/BK* PR9 ....10 D3
Brook Farm Cl *ORM* L39 ....30 D1
Brookfield Cl *SKEL* WN8 ....39 E1
Brookhouse Rd *ORM* L39 ....26 C4
Brooklands *ORM* L39 ....27 E4
Brooklands Dr
WGNW/BIL/OR WN5 ....39 G3
Brooklands Gv *BRSC* L40 ....23 G4
Brooklands Rd *SKEL* WN8 ....39 F1
Brook La *ORM* L39 ....30 D1
Brookside *BRSC* L40 ....21 F4
Brookside Rd *STHP* PR8 ....13 G4
Brooks Rd *FMBY* L37 ....28 D4
Brook St *CHTN/BK* PR9 ....6 A3
Brooks Wy *FMBY* L37 ....28 D4
Broom Cl *BRSC* L40 ....23 G3
Broome Cl *STHP* PR8 ....13 F2
Broome Rd *STHP* PR8 ....13 F2
Broughton Av *STHP* PR8 ....13 H1
Brown Edge Cl *STHP* PR8 ....14 C3
Brows Cl *FMBY* L37 ....29 E3
Brows La *FMBY* L37 ....29 E3
Bryony Cl *WGNW/BIL/OR* WN5 ....39 G3
Buckfast Dr *FMBY* L37 ....29 H4
Buckingham Gv *FMBY* L37 ....29 E4
Bull Cop *FMBY* L37 ....29 G5
Bullens La *BRSC* L40 ....20 B1
Burlington Av *FMBY* L37 ....29 H3
Burlington Rd *STHP* PR8 ....12 D2
Burnley Rd *STHP* PR8 ....19 E5
Burscough Rd *STHP* PR8 ....27 E5
Burscough St *ORM* L39 ....26 D5
Burwell Av *FMBY* L37 ....28 D5
Bury Rd *STHP* PR8 ....13 E2
Bushby's La *FMBY* L37 ....28 C4
Bushby's Pk *FMBY* L37 ....28 C4
Butterfield Gdns *ORM* L39 ....30 C2
Buttermere Cl *FMBY* L37 ....28 D3
Butts La *STHP* PR8 ....10 B5
Byland Cl *FMBY* L37 ....29 H4
Byrom St *CHTN/BK* PR9 ....10 B4
Byron Cl *FMBY* L37 ....29 F2

C

Cabin La *CHTN/BK* PR9 ....6 C4
Cable St *CHTN/BK* PR9 ....3 G3
FMBY L37 ....29 G2
Caister Cl *SKEL* WN8 ....34 A5
Calder Av *ORM* L39 ....30 D1
Camberley Cl *STHP* PR8 ....8 C5
Cambridge Ar *STHP* PR8 ....3 G4
Cambridge Av *CHTN/BK* PR9 ....5 F5
Cambridge Gdns *CHTN/BK* PR9 .....5 F5
Cambridge Rd *CHTN/BK* PR9 ....10 A1
FMBY L37 ....28 D5
SKEL WN8 ....32 D4
WGNW/BIL/OR WN5 ....35 H5
Cambridge Wks *STHP* PR8 ....3 G4
Canal Bank *BRSC* L40 * 22 C1
Canalside *BRSC* L40 ....21 F4
Canning Rd *CHTN/BK* PR9 ....10 C3
Canterbury Cl *FMBY* L37 ....29 H4
STHP PR8 ....12 D1
Cantlow Fold *STHP* PR8 ....18 C4
Capilano Pk *STHP* PR8 ....30 B5
Cardiff St *SKEL* WN8 ....32 C4
Cardigan Rd *STHP* PR8 ....12 D4
Carfield *SKEL* WN8 ....38 B2
Carisbrooke Dr *CHTN/BK* PR9 ......10 B1
Carlisle Rd *STHP* PR8 ....13 E3
Carlton Av *SKEL* WN8 ....38 D1
Carlton Rd *STHP* PR8 ....19 E2
Carmel Cl *ORM* L39 ....30 C3
Carnarvon Rd *STHP* PR8 ....12 D4
Carnoustie Ct *STHP* PR8 ....9 B5
Carr House La *HTWN* L38 ....41 F3
Carr La *STHP* PR8 ....19 H1
Carr Moss La *STHP* PR8 ....19 G4
Carroll Crs *ORM* L39 ....30 B5
Carr's Crs *FMBY* L37 ....28 D5
Carr's Crs West *FMBY* L37 ....28 D5
Carr Side La *SFTN* L29 ....41 H4
Carrwood Pk *STHP* PR8 ....13 F2
Cartmel Cl *FMBY* L37 ....14 B2
Cartmel Dr *FMBY* L37 ....29 H4
Carvel Wy *BRSC* L40 ....23 G4
Cascades *SKEL* WN8 * 37 H1
Castle Dr *FMBY* L37 ....29 F5
Castlehey *SKEL* WN8 ....38 B2

Castle St *CHTN/BK* PR9 ....3 H3
Castle Wk *STHP* PR8 ....2 E6
Catharine's La *ORM* L39 ....31 E3
Caton Cl *CHTN/BK* PR9 ....5 F3
Cat Tail La *STHP* PR8 ....15 G4
Catterick Fold *STHP* PR8 ....14 B2
Caunce Av *ORM* L39 ....7 E1
The Causeway *CHTN/BK* PR9 ....6 A2
Cavendish St *STHP* PR8 ....12 D2
Cedar Crs *ORM* L39 ....30 B1
Cedar Dr *FMBY* L37 ....28 C5
Cedar Gv *SKEL* WN8 ....32 D4
Cedar St *STHP* PR8 ....13 G1
Cemetery Rd *STHP* PR8 ....9 G5
Central Av *STHP* PR8 ....12 D5
Chambres Rd *STHP* PR8 ....9 H5
Chambres Rd North *STHP* PR8 ...9 H4
Chandley Cl *STHP* PR8 ....18 C3
Chapelhouse Wk *FMBY* L37 .....29 G3
Chapel La *BRSC* L40 ....23 F5
  CHTN/BK PR9 ....7 F1
  FMBY L37 ....29 F3
Chapel Ms *ORM* L39 ....30 D1
Chapel St *ORM* L39 ....27 E5
  STHP PR8 ....3 G4
Charles Av *STHP* PR8 ....19 G2
Charlesbye Av *ORM* L39 ....27 F4
Chartwell Rd *STHP* PR8 ....18 D2
Chase Cl *STHP* PR8 ....12 D1
Chase Heys *CHTN/BK* PR9 ......10 B1
Chatsworth Rd *STHP* PR8 ....18 C2
Cheapside *FMBY* L37 ....29 G4
Cheltenham Wy *STHP* PR8 ....14 B1
Chequer Cl *SKEL* WN8 ....38 C3
Chequer La *SKEL* WN8 ....38 C2
Cheriton Pk *STHP* PR8 ....9 F5
Cherrycroft *SKEL* WN8 ....38 B2
Cherry Gn *ORM* L39 ....30 A4
Cherry Gv *BRSC* L40 ....23 F1
Cherry Rd *STHP* PR8 ....25 F1
Cherry Tree La *BRSC* L40 ....21 E4
  ORM L39 ....30 A4
Cheshire Lines Pth *ORM* L39 ...25 H5
Chester Av *CHTN/BK* PR9 ....10 B1
Chesterfield Cl *STHP* PR8 ....18 D4
Chesterfield Rd *STHP* PR8 ....18 D4
Chester Rd *CHTN/BK* PR9 ......10 B2
Chestnut Ct *ORM* L39 ....27 E4
Chestnut Gra *ORM* L39 ....30 C2
Chestnut St *STHP* PR8 ....13 G1
Chestnut Wy *FMBY* L37 ....28 C5
Chiltern Rd *STHP* PR8 ....18 C2
Chindit Cl *FMBY* L37 ....28 D4
Chipping Av *STHP* PR8 ....18 C3
Chislett Cl *BRSC* L40 * 23 E3
Chorley Cl *CHTN/BK* PR9 ....6 C2
Christines Crs *BRSC* L40 ....23 E3
Church Cl *CHTN/BK* PR9 ....10 C2
  FMBY L37 ....29 G3
Church Close Ct *FMBY* L37 * ...29 G3
Church Dr *WGNW/BIL/OR* WN5 ...39 G3
Church Flds *BRSC* L40 ....20 D1
  ORM L39 ....26 D5
Churchfields *STHP* PR8 ....12 D2
Churchgate *CHTN/BK* PR9 ......10 B1
Churchgate Ms *CHTN/BK* PR9 ..10 C1
Church Gn *FMBY* L37 ....28 C4
  SKEL WN8 ....33 E4
Church Hill Rd *ORM* L39 ....26 C4
Churchill Av *CHTN/BK* PR9 ....5 F5
Church Rd *CHTN/BK* PR9 ....7 E1
  FMBY L37 ....29 G2
  SKEL WN8 ....33 E4
Church St *CHTN/BK* PR9 ....3 J3
  ORM L39 ....26 D5
  SKEL WN8 ....39 F1
  WGNW/BIL/OR WN5 ....39 G3
Church Wy *FMBY* L37 ....28 C4
Cinnamon Brow *SKEL* WN8 .....39 F2
Claremont Av *STHP* PR8 ....13 E1
Claremont Dr *ORM* L39 ....30 C2
Claremont Gdns *STHP* PR8 ......13 E1
Claremont Rd *STHP* PR8 ....13 E1
Clarence Rd *STHP* PR8 ....13 E1
Clarkfield Cl *BRSC* L40 ....23 G4
Clay Brow Rd *SKEL* WN8 ....38 B2
Clayton Gdns *BRSC* L40 ....23 F3
Clayton Ms *SKEL* WN8 ....32 C4
Clayton St *SKEL* WN8 ....32 C4
Clegg St *SKEL* WN8 ....32 C4
Clengers Brow
  CHTN/BK PR9 ....5 G4
Cleveleys Av *CHTN/BK* PR9 ......5 G3
Cleveleys Rd *CHTN/BK* PR9 ......5 G4
Cleve Wy *FMBY* L37 ....29 H4
Clifford Rd *STHP* PR8 ....13 E4
Cliff Rd *CHTN/BK* PR9 ....4 D5
Clifton Dr *FMBY* L37 ....29 G1
  STHP PR8 ....10 B4

Clinning Rd *STHP* PR8 ....13 E3
Clive Ldg *STHP* PR8 ....12 D3
Clive Rd *STHP* PR8 ....12 D4
The Cloisters *FMBY* L37 * 29 F3
The Close *CHTN/BK* PR9 ....7 E2
  HTWN L38 ....41 F4
Clough Av *BRSC* L40 ....23 G3
Clovelly Dr *STHP* PR8 ....12 C5
Clucas Gdns *ORM* L39 ....26 D4
Clyffes Farm Cl *BRSC* L40 ....21 E1
Coach House Ct *BRSC* L40 ......23 F4
Coal Pit La *ORM* L39 ....36 B4
Coastal Rd *STHP* PR8 ....18 C2
Coastline Ms *CHTN/BK* PR9 ......5 E3
Cobden Rd *CHTN/BK* PR9 ....10 B4
Cockle Dick's La *CHTN/BK* PR9 ...5 E5
Colburne Cl *BRSC* L40 ....23 G2
Colchester Rd *STHP* PR8 ....14 B3
Cole Crs *ORM* L39 ....30 B5
Colinmander Gdns *ORM* L39 ...30 B2
Colinton *SKEL* WN8 ....38 B1
College Av *FMBY* L37 ....29 E2
College Cl *FMBY* L37 ....28 D2
  STHP PR8 ....13 E2
College Pth *FMBY* L37 ....28 D1
College Rd *SKEL* WN8 ....35 E4
Collisdene Rd
  WGNW/BIL/OR WN5 ....39 G2
Common La *CHTN/BK* PR9 ....7 F5
Compton Rd *STHP* PR8 ....13 F2
Conifer Ct *FMBY* L37 ....29 F4
Coniston Rd *FMBY* L37 ....28 D4
Convent Cl *ORM* L39 ....30 C3
Conyers Av *STHP* PR8 ....12 D2
Coppice Leys *FMBY* L37 ....29 E3
Cornbrook *SKEL* WN8 ....38 B1
Cornwall Wy *STHP* PR8 ....24 D1
Coronation Av *FMBY* L37 ....29 G4
Coronation Wk *STHP* PR8 ....2 E4
Cosgate Cl *WGNW/BIL/OR* WN5 ...39 H3
Cottage Cl *ORM* L39 ....30 C1
Cottage La *ORM* L39 ....30 C1
Cottage Ms *ORM* L39 ....26 C5
Cotton Dr *ORM* L39 ....26 C4
Cottys Brow *CHTN/BK* PR9 ....5 F4
Coudray Rd *CHTN/BK* PR9 .....10 A1
County Rd *ORM* L39 ....26 C3
Courtfield *ORM* L39 ....26 C3
Courtgreen *ORM* L39 ....26 C3
Court Ms *CHTN/BK* PR9 * 10 C1
Court Rd *CHTN/BK* PR9 ....3 J2
Covertside Rd *STHP* PR8 ....14 C3
Coyford Dr *CHTN/BK* PR9 ....5 G3
Crabtree Cl *BRSC* L40 ....23 E3
Crabtree La *BRSC* L40 ....22 D2
Crediton Av *CHTN/BK* PR9 ....5 H2
Crescent Av *FMBY* L37 ....29 F1
Crescent Gn *ORM* L39 ....30 A4
Crescent Rd *STHP* PR8 ....12 D2
The Crescent *CHTN/BK* PR9 ......6 A4
Cricket Pth *FMBY* L37 ....29 F1
  STHP PR8 ....12 D2
Crockleford Av *STHP* PR8 ....14 A2
Croft Av *BRSC* L40 ....23 G4
  WGNW/BIL/OR WN5 ....39 G3
Croft Heys *ORM* L39 ....30 A4
Croftlands
  WGNW/BIL/OR WN5 ....39 G4
Croftson Av *ORM* L39 ....27 E3
The Croft
  WGNW/BIL/OR WN5 ....39 G4
Cromer Rd *STHP* PR8 ....12 C3
Cromfield *ORM* L39 ....30 B3
Cromwell Ct *ORM* L39 ....30 B3
Cropton Rd *FMBY* L37 ....29 F3
Cross Barn La *HTWN* L38 ....41 F5
Crossens Wy *CHTN/BK* PR9 ....6 A1
Crossfield St *SKEL* WN8 ....33 H5
Cross Green Cl *FMBY* L37 ....29 G4
Crosshall Brow *BRSC* L40 ....31 H1
  ORM L39 ....31 H1
Cross La
  WGNW/BIL/OR WN5 ....39 G5
Cross St *STHP* PR8 ....3 G4
The Cross *HTWN* L38 ....41 E4
Croston's Brow *CHTN/BK* PR9 ...5 F4
Crowland Cl *CHTN/BK* PR9 .....10 C4
Crowland St *CHTN/BK* PR9 .....10 C4
Crowland Wy *FMBY* L37 ....29 H4
Crow La *SKEL* WN8 ....34 C2
Crown Cl *FMBY* L37 ....29 G4
Croyde Cl *CHTN/BK* PR9 ....5 H2
Culshaw Wy *SKEL* WN8 ....20 D1
Cumberland Rd *STHP* PR8 ....19 H5
Curzon Rd *STHP* PR8 ....10 A5
Cygnet Cl *ORM* L39 ....30 B3
Cypress Rd *STHP* PR8 ....10 A4

D

Dailton Rd *SKEL* WN8 ....38 D1
Daisy Wy *STHP* PR8 ....13 F3
Dam Wood La *BRSC* L40 ....21 F3
Danbers *SKEL* WN8 ....38 C2
Daneway *STHP* PR8 ....18 D2
Daniels La *SKEL* WN8 ....37 H1
Daresbury Av *STHP* PR8 ....18 C3
Darfield *SKEL* WN8 ....38 C1
Dark La *BRSC* L40 ....27 G4
Davenham Rd *FMBY* L37 ....29 F2
Dawlish Dr *CHTN/BK* PR9 ....5 G2
Dawson Av *CHTN/BK* PR9 ....6 A2
Dawson Rd *ORM* L39 ....27 E3
Daybrook *SKEL* WN8 ....38 C2
Dayfield *SKEL* WN8 ....38 D1
Dean Cl *SKEL* WN8 ....39 F1
Deans Ct *STHP* PR8 ....29 F1
Deansgate La *FMBY* L37 ....29 H1
Deansgate La North *FMBY* L37 ...24 C5
Dean Wood Av
  WGNW/BIL/OR WN5 ....35 H4
De-Haviland Wy *SKEL* WN8 .....34 B5
Delamere Rd *SKEL* WN8 ....33 E3
  STHP PR8 ....18 D3
Delamere Wy *SKEL* WN8 ....38 D1
The Dell *SKEL* WN8 ....39 E1
Delph Common Rd *ORM* L39 ...30 A4
Delph Dr *BRSC* L40 ....23 G3
Delph La *FMBY* L37 ....28 C3
  ORM L39 ....30 A5
Delph Park Av *ORM* L39 ....30 A5
Delphside Cl
  WGNW/BIL/OR WN5 ....39 G3
Delphside Rd
  WGNW/BIL/OR WN5 ....39 F3
Delph Top *ORM* L39 ....27 F4
Denbigh Av *CHTN/BK* PR9 ....5 F4
Denholme *SKEL* WN8 ....38 C1
Denmark Rd *CHTN/BK* PR9 ....5 G5
Derby Hill Crs *ORM* L39 ....27 F5
Derby Hill Rd *ORM* L39 ....27 F5
Derby Rd *CHTN/BK* PR9 ....3 J4
  FMBY L37 ....29 G2
  SKEL WN8 ....32 B5
Derby St *ORM* L39 ....27 E5
Derby St West *ORM* L39 ....26 D5
Derwent Av *CHTN/BK* PR9 ......10 B1
  FMBY L37 ....29 E2
Devon Av *SKEL* WN8 ....39 E2
Devon Farm Wy *FMBY* L37 ......29 H3
Devonshire Rd
  CHTN/BK PR9 ....10 C3
Dewberry Flds *SKEL* WN8 ....39 F3
Dicconson Wy *ORM* L39 * 31 F1
Dickinson Cl *FMBY* L37 ....29 F4
Dickinson Rd *FMBY* L37 ....29 F4
Digmoor Dr *SKEL* WN8 ....37 G1
Digmoor Rd *SKEL* WN8 ....37 H1
Dingle Av *SKEL* WN8 ....35 E5
Dingle Cl *ORM* L39 ....30 B4
Dingle Rd *SKEL* WN8 ....39 E1
Dinorwic Rd *STHP* PR8 ....13 E2
Ditchfield *FMBY* L37 ....29 G4
Dobbs Dr *FMBY* L37 ....29 G2
Dodworth Av *STHP* PR8 ....10 A5
Dolly's La *CHTN/BK* PR9 ....11 F2
Dorchester Rd *SKEL* WN8 ....38 D1
Doric Gn
  WGNW/BIL/OR WN5 ....39 G5
Dorset Av *STHP* PR8 ....18 D5
Douglas Av *SKEL* WN8 ....39 E1
Douglas Dr *ORM* L39 ....26 C3
Douglas Rd
  CHTN/BK PR9 ....10 A3
Dover Rd *STHP* PR8 ....12 D3
Dragon Cl *SKEL* WN8 ....34 B5
Drake Cl *ORM* L39 ....30 D3
Drewitt Crs *CHTN/BK* PR9 ....6 A3
Drummersdale La
  BRSC L40 ....16 B4
Duke Av *STHP* PR8 ....18 D4
Duke St *FMBY* L37 ....29 E4
  STHP PR8 ....2 E5
Dukes Wy *FMBY* L37 ....29 F4
Duke's Wood La
  SKEL WN8 ....34 A3
Dunbar Crs *STHP* PR8 ....12 D5
Dunbar Rd *STHP* PR8 ....12 C4
Dunes Dr *FMBY* L37 ....28 C2
Dunkirk Rd *STHP* PR8 ....12 D3
Dunlop Av *STHP* PR8 ....25 E1
Dunster Rd *STHP* PR8 ....12 C5
Durham St *SKEL* WN8 ....33 H5
Dyers La *ORM* L39 ....30 D1

E

Eamont Av *CHTN/BK* PR9 ....5 F
Earlswood *SKEL* WN8 ....34 B
Easby Cl *FMBY* L37 ....29 G
Easedale Dr *STHP* PR8 ....18 D
Eastbank St *STHP* PR8 ....3 G
Eastbourne Rd *STHP* PR8 ....13 E
East Leigh *SKEL* WN8 ....34 B
East Md *ORM* L39 ....30 A
East St *CHTN/BK* PR9 ....10 B
Eavesdale *SKEL* WN8 ....34 B
Eccles Rd *FMBY* L37 ....28 D
Eden Av *CHTN/BK* PR9 ....5 F
Edenfield Cl *STHP* PR8 ....14 A
Edenhurst *SKEL* WN8 ....34 B
Edenhurst Cl *FMBY* L37 ....28 C
Edenhurst Dr *FMBY* L37 ....28 C
Edge Hall Rd
  WGNW/BIL/OR WN5 ....39 J
Edgley Dr *ORM* L39 ....27 H
Edinburgh Rd *FMBY* L37 ....29 G
Egerton *SKEL* WN8 ....34 B
Eight Acre La *FMBY* L37 ....24 D
Elbow La *FMBY* L37 ....29 E
Eldons Cft *STHP* PR8 ....19 F
Elizabeth Av *STHP* PR8 ....19 G
Ellerbrook Dr *BRSC* L40 ....23 G
Ellerbrook Wy *ORM* L39 ....26 D
Elmcroft La *HTWN* L38 ....40 B
Elmdale Cl *FMBY* L37 ....28 D
Elm Dr *FMBY* L37 ....28 C
Elmers Gn *SKEL* WN8 ....34 A
Elmer's Green La *SKEL* WN8 .....33 H
Elmers Wood Rd *SKEL* WN8 .....34 A
Elm Gv *SKEL* WN8 * ....32 D
Elm Park Dr *STHP* PR8 ....19 G
Elm Pl *ORM* L39 ....30 A
Elmridge *SKEL* WN8 ....34 B
Elm Rd *BRSC* L40 ....23 G
  STHP PR8 ....13 G
Elmstead *SKEL* WN8 ....34 B
Elmwood *SKEL* WN8 ....33 H
Elson Rd *FMBY* L37 ....28 D
Elswick *SKEL* WN8 ....38 B
Elswick Rd *CHTN/BK* PR9 ....10 B
Elvington Rd *HTWN* L38 ....40 C
Ely Ms *CHTN/BK* PR9 ....10 C
Emerson Cl *HTWN* L38 ....40 C
Emmanuel Rd *CHTN/BK* PR9 .....5 H
Emmsix *BRSC* L40 ....21 E
Ennerdale *SKEL* WN8 ....28 D
Ennerdale Cl *FMBY* L37 ....28 D
Ennerdale Dr *ORM* L39 ....30 C
Ennerdale Rd *FMBY* L37 ....28 D
Enstone *SKEL* WN8 ....34 C
Ericson Dr *STHP* PR8 ....9 F
Eskbank *SKEL* WN8 ....33 H
Eskbrook *SKEL* WN8 ....33 H
Eskdale *SKEL* WN8 ....33 H
Eskdale Av *ORM* L39 ....30 C
Eskdale Cl *FMBY* L37 ....28 D
Eskdale Dr *FMBY* L37 ....28 D
Esplanade *STHP* PR8 ....2 B
Essex Rd *STHP* PR8 ....13 E
Ettington Dr *STHP* PR8 ....18 C
Evenwood *SKEL* WN8 ....34 B
Evenwood Ct *SKEL* WN8 * ....33 H
Everard Cl *BRSC* L40 ....20 D
Everard Rd *STHP* PR8 ....28 D
The Evergreens *FMBY* L37 ....28 D
Eversham Cl *CHTN/BK* PR9 ....7 F
Eversley *SKEL* WN8 ....34 B
Everton Rd *STHP* PR8 ....13 E
Evington *SKEL* WN8 ....34 B
Exmoor Cl *CHTN/BK* PR9 ....5 F

F

Fairburn *SKEL* WN8 ....33 H
Fairfield Cl *ORM* L39 ....26 D
Fairfield Dr *ORM* L39 ....26 D
Fairfield Rd *STHP* PR8 ....19 G
Fairhaven *SKEL* WN8 ....33 H
Fairhaven Rd *CHTN/BK* PR9 ......5 G
Fairlie *SKEL* WN8 ....33 H
Fairstead *SKEL* WN8 ....33 H
Fairway *CHTN/BK* PR9 ....4 D
Fairways Ct *FMBY* L37 ....28 C
The Fairways *SKEL* WN8 ....33 H
Falkland *SKEL* WN8 ....33 H
Falkland Rd *FMBY* L37 ....9 F
Fareham Dr *CHTN/BK* PR9 ....7 F
Farley La *SKEL* WN8 ....34 C
Farm Cl *CHTN/BK* PR9 ....10 D

rm Meadow Rd
 WGNW/BIL/OR WN5 ....39 H3
rnborough Rd STHP PR8 ....12 D5
rrington Dr ORM L39 ....26 D4
ulkner Cl STHP PR8 ....19 E3
ulkner Gdns STHP PR8 ....19 E2
wcett SKEL WN8 ....33 G2
llview CHTN/BK PR9 ....6 B1
lstead SKEL WN8 ....33 G3
ltons SKEL WN8 ....33 G3
nney Ct SKEL WN8 ....33 H4
rn Cl SKEL WN8 ....32 D4
rndale SKEL WN8 ....33 G3
rnhurst Ga ORM L39 ....30 A3
rnley Rd STHP PR8 ....9 E5
rny Knoll Rd RNFD/HAY WA11 ..37 E4
rry Side La CHTN/BK PR9 ....6 A2
eld Cl BRSC L40 ....23 G4
eldlands STHP PR8 ....14 C3
eldview SKEL WN8 ....38 D1
eld Wk ORM L39 ....27 G5
ndon SKEL WN8 ....33 H4
ne Jane's Wy CHTN/BK PR9 ....10 D2
rbeck SKEL WN8 ....33 H4
rs Cl FMBY L37 ....28 D1
rs Crs FMBY L37 ....28 D1
rs Link FMBY L37 ....28 D2
r St STHP PR8 ....10 B4
rswood Rd SKEL WN8 ....32 B1
r Tree Cl SKEL WN8 ....38 A1
rwood SKEL WN8 ....34 A2
sher Dr CHTN/BK PR9 ....10 B3
 WGNW/BIL/OR WN5 ....39 H2
shermans Cl FMBY L37 ....24 A5
sh La BRSC L40 ....17 H2
amstead SKEL WN8 ....33 H4
axfield Rd FMBY L37 ....29 G3
axfields BRSC L40 ....23 G5
ax La BRSC L40 ....23 G5
axton SKEL WN8 ....33 H4
eetwood Cl CHTN/BK PR9 ....5 F4
eetwood Crs CHTN/BK PR9 ....7 E1
eetwood Dr CHTN/BK PR9 ....7 E1
eetwood Rd CHTN/BK PR9 ....9 G1
etcher's Dr BRSC L40 ....23 F3
mby SKEL WN8 ....34 A4
odgates Rd HTWN L38 ....40 A2
ordon SKEL WN8 ....34 A4
lkestone Rd STHP PR8 ....14 A2
rdham Cl STHP PR8 ....14 A2
rest Dr SKEL WN8 ....33 H2
rest Rd STHP PR8 ....9 H4
rmby Br FMBY L37 ....29 E4
rmby By-Pass FMBY L37 ....24 D4
rmby Flds FMBY L37 ....29 G4
rmby Gdns FMBY L37 ....29 F2
rmby St FMBY L37 ....29 G1
ster FMBY L37 ....28 D4
sters Cl CHTN/BK PR9 ....10 D2
sters Green Rd SKEL WN8 ....33 H3
ul La CHTN/BK PR9 ....10 C5
 STHP PR8 ....14 C1
untains Wy FMBY L37 ....29 G2
xdale Cl STHP PR8 ....14 A2
xfold SKEL WN8 ....34 A2
xhill Cl FMBY L37 ....28 C3
xwood Cl
 WGNW/BIL/OR WN5 ....39 H3
ailey Cl STHP PR8 ....19 E4
eckleton Rd CHTN/BK PR9 ....5 F3
eshfield Rd FMBY L37 ....29 E4
iars Wk FMBY L37 ....29 H4
lwood Av STHP PR8 ....13 H1
nchal Av FMBY L37 ....28 D5
rness Av FMBY L37 ....29 G4
 ORM L39 ....30 D1
rness Cl STHP PR8 ....18 D5
rnival Dr BRSC L40 ....23 E3
lde Rd CHTN/BK PR9 ....5 F3

G

briel Cl SKEL WN8 ....35 F2
insborough Rd STHP PR8 ....12 C2
lloway Dr SKEL WN8 ....39 E2
ntley Av WGNW/BIL/OR WN5 ......39 G4
ntley Crs WGNW/BIL/OR WN5 ...39 G4
ntley Rd WGNW/BIL/OR WN5 .....39 G4
nton Cl STHP PR8 ....14 A1
rdiners Pl SKEL WN8 ....32 D5
rdner Rd FMBY L37 ....29 G3
rnett Gdns ORM L39 ....30 D1
rnett Rd SKEL WN8 ....37 F1
rrick Pde STHP PR8 ....2 E5
rstang Rd CHTN/BK PR9 ....5 F3
thurst Rd
 WGNW/BIL/OR WN5 ....35 H4

Gaw's Hill Vw ORM L39 ....30 A2
George Dr STHP PR8 ....19 G3
George's Ter
 WGNW/BIL/OR WN5 ....39 G3
Georgian Pl FMBY L37 ....29 E5
Gerrard Pl SKEL WN8 ....37 E1
Gilbert Rd BRSC L40 ....22 C3
Gillibrands Rd SKEL WN8 ....37 F1
Gladden Pl SKEL WN8 ....32 D5
Gladstone Rd CHTN/BK PR9 ....10 B4
Glaisdale Dr STHP PR8 ....14 B2
Glamis Dr CHTN/BK PR9 ....5 H4
Glebe Pl STHP PR8 ....3 G3
Glebe Rd SKEL WN8 ....37 F1
Glenburn Rd SKEL WN8 ....32 D1
Glencoyne Dr CHTN/BK PR9 ....5 H2
Glendale Wy FMBY L37 ....29 F4
Gleneagles Dr STHP PR8 ....18 D5
Glenmarsh Wy FMBY L37 ....29 H3
Glenpark Dr CHTN/BK PR9 ....5 H1
Glenrose Ter STHP PR8 ....9 E5
Glenroyd Dr BRSC L40 ....23 F3
Gloucester Rd STHP PR8 ....2 D7
Golf Rd FMBY L37 ....28 D1
Gordon Av SKEL WN8 ....9 C1
Gordon St CHTN/BK PR9 ....9 G1
Gore Dr ORM L39 ....30 D2
Gores La FMBY L37 ....29 E1
Gorsefield FMBY L37 ....24 C5
Gorse Wy SKEL WN8 ....28 C2
Gorsey La HTWN L38 ....40 C5
Gorsey Pl SKEL WN8 ....37 F1
Gorst La BRSC L40 ....22 A1
Gorsuch La BRSC L40 ....20 B4
Gosforth Rd CHTN/BK PR9 ....10 B2
Gower Gdns BRSC L40 ....23 G4
Graburn Rd FMBY L37 ....29 F2
Grafton Dr STHP PR8 ....19 G3
Granby Cl CHTN/BK PR9 ....5 F4
Grange Av CHTN/BK PR9 ....10 A2
Grange La FMBY L37 ....29 E1
Grange Rd CHTN/BK PR9 ....10 A3
The Grange CHTN/BK PR9 ....6 A4
Grantham Cl SKEL WN8 ....13 E4
Grantham Rd STHP PR8 ....13 E4
Granton Cl FMBY L37 ....29 E3
Granville Cl ORM L39 ....30 A4
Granville Pk ORM L39 ....30 A5
Granville Pk West ORM L39 ....30 A5
Granville Rd STHP PR8 ....12 B2
Grasmere Av SKEL WN8 ....35 E5
Grasmere Rd FMBY L37 ....28 D3
Gratton Pl SKEL WN8 ....33 F5
Gravel La CHTN/BK PR9 ....6 D2
Greaves Cl CHTN/BK PR9 ....9 H4
Greaves Hall Av CHTN/BK PR9 .....7 E3
Greenbank ORM L39 ....30 B3
Greenbank Av
 WGNW/BIL/OR WN5 ....39 G5
Greenbank Dr STHP PR8 ....12 C3
Greenfield Rd STHP PR8 ....15 E4
Greenford Cl
 WGNW/BIL/OR WN5 ....39 G2
Greenford Rd STHP PR8 ....19 E4
Greenhey Rd SKEL WN8 ....33 E5
Greenings La CHTN/BK PR9 ....16 C2
Green La BRSC L40 ....7 G3
 CHTN/BK PR9 ....24 B5
 FMBY L37 ....26 A4
 ORM L39 ....26 A4
 WGNW/BIL/OR WN5 ....39 H3
Green Lane Av ORM L39 * 26 D4
Greenlea Cl WGNW/BIL/OR WN5 ..39 G3
Greenloon's Dr FMBY L37 ....28 C3
Greenloon's Wk FMBY L37 ....28 C4
Greenslate Ct
 WGNW/BIL/OR WN5 ....39 G5
Greenslate Rd
 WGNW/BIL/OR WN5 ....39 H5
Green Wk STHP PR8 ....19 H3
Greenway Av SKEL WN8 ....37 G1
Greenway Cl SKEL WN8 ....32 D3
Greenways WGNW/BIL/OR WN5 ..39 G5
Greenwood Cl ORM L39 ....30 B4
Greetby Hl ORM L39 ....27 F5
Greetby Pl SKEL WN8 ....33 F5
Gregson's Av FMBY L37 ....29 F3
Greyfriars Rd STHP PR8 ....18 D2
Greystokes ORM L39 ....30 C3
Griffiths Dr CHTN/BK PR9 ....10 B2
Grimrod Pl SKEL WN8 ....37 F1
Grimshaw La ORM L39 ....26 D4
Grimshaw Rd SKEL WN8 ....33 G5
Grinstead Cl STHP PR8 ....12 D4
Grisedale Cl FMBY L37 ....29 E3
Grosvenor Cl STHP PR8 ....12 D2
Grosvenor Gdns STHP PR8 ....12 D2
Grosvenor Pl STHP PR8 ....12 D2
Grosvenor Rd STHP PR8 ....12 C1

Grove Pk CHTN/BK PR9 ....10 B1
 ORM L39 ....27 E3
Grove Rd SKEL WN8 ....35 E5
Grove St STHP PR8 ....9 E5
Grove Ter STHP PR8 ....9 E5
Grovewood STHP PR8 ....12 C1
Grundy Cl STHP PR8 ....10 A5
Guildford Rd STHP PR8 ....13 E5
Guinea Hall Cl CHTN/BK PR9 ....7 E2
Guinea Hall La CHTN/BK PR9 ....7 E2

H

Hadstock Av FMBY L37 ....28 D5
Haig Av STHP PR8 ....10 A5
Halifax Rd STHP PR8 ....19 E3
Hallbridge Gdns SKEL WN8 ....35 E5
Hall Brow Cl ORM L39 ....31 C1
Hallcroft SKEL WN8 ....33 H3
Hall Gn SKEL WN8 ....39 E1
Hall Green Cl SKEL WN8 ....39 E1
Hall La HTWN L38 ....41 G3
Hallmoor Cl ORM L39 ....30 C3
Hall Rd BRSC L40 ....21 E2
Hall St CHTN/BK PR9 ....3 K4
Halsall Buildings CHTN/BK PR9 ....3 K2
Halsall La FMBY L37 ....3 F1
 ORM L39 ....26 C4
Halsall Rd STHP PR8 ....13 E5
Hampton Rd FMBY L37 ....29 E5
 STHP PR8 ....13 F1
 STHP PR8 ....3 K6
Hansby Cl SKEL WN8 ....34 B5
Hanstock WGNW/BIL/OR WN5 ....39 H3
Hants La ORM L39 ....26 D4
Harbury Av STHP PR8 ....18 C4
Hardacre St ORM L39 ....27 E4
Harding Rd BRSC L40 ....23 E3
Harebell Cl FMBY L37 ....29 F5
Hares La SKEL WN8 ....15 F4
Harewood Av STHP PR8 ....19 E2
Hargreaves St STHP PR8 ....3 K5
Harington Cl FMBY L37 ....28 C3
Harington Gn FMBY L37 ....28 D3
Harington Rd FMBY L37 ....28 C2
Harrod Dr STHP PR8 ....12 C2
Harrogate Wy CHTN/BK PR9 ....6 A1
Harsnips SKEL WN8 ....33 H3
Harswell Cl WGNW/BIL/OR WN5 ..39 H3
Hartland Av CHTN/BK PR9 ....5 H3
Hartley Crs STHP PR8 ....12 D2
Hartley Rd STHP PR8 ....12 D3
Hartshead SKEL WN8 ....33 H3
Hart's La SKEL WN8 ....34 C5
Hart St STHP PR8 ....9 H4
Hart Street Br CHTN/BK PR9 ....9 H4
Hartwood Rd CHTN/BK PR9 ....9 H4
Harvington Dr STHP PR8 ....18 C3
Haslam Dr ORM L39 ....26 C3
Hastings Rd STHP PR8 ....12 C4
Hatfield Rd STHP PR8 ....19 E2
Haven Brow ORM L39 ....30 B5
Hawesside St CHTN/BK PR9 ....3 H4
Hawksclough SKEL WN8 ....33 H3
Hawkshead St CHTN/BK PR9 ....9 H3
 CHTN/BK PR9 ....3 K2
Hawksworth Cl FMBY L37 ....24 C5
Hawksworth Dr FMBY L37 ....24 C5
Hawthorn Av BRSC L40 ....23 G3
Hawthorn Crs SKEL WN8 ....32 D4
Hawthorne Crs FMBY L37 ....29 G4
Hawthorne Gv CHTN/BK PR9 ....10 B3
Hayfield Rd ORM L39 ....26 B3
Hazelbank Gdns FMBY L37 * 29 E1
Hazel Gv STHP PR8 ....10 A3
Hazel La SKEL WN8 ....33 G1
Hazelwood Av BRSC L40 ....23 F3
Hazlehurst Cl FMBY L37 ....28 C4
Headingly Av SKEL WN8 ....32 B3
Heanor Dr STHP PR8 ....14 B2
Heather Cl BRSC L40 ....23 F3
 FMBY L37 ....29 H1
 STHP PR8 ....25 F1
Heatherlea Cl SKEL WN8 ....39 E1
Heatherways FMBY L37 ....24 C5
Heathey La STHP PR8 ....14 B5
Heathfield Cl FMBY L37 ....24 C5
Heathfield Rd STHP PR8 ....19 G3
Heathgate SKEL WN8 ....33 H3
Heaton Cl BRSC L40 ....23 E3
 SKEL WN8 ....38 D1
Heatons Bridge Rd BRSC L40 ......21 H4
Hedgeview BRSC L40 ....21 F4
Helmsdale SKEL WN8 ....33 H3
Helston Cl CHTN/BK PR9 ....5 H2
Henley Dr CHTN/BK PR9 ....10 A1
Hereford Gv SKEL WN8 ....39 E1

Hereford Rd CHTN/BK PR9 ....10 B3
Hesketh Av CHTN/BK PR9 ....7 E1
Hesketh Dr STHP PR8 ....5 E5
Hesketh Rd BRSC L40 ....23 E3
 CHTN/BK PR9 ....4 D4
Heskin La ORM L39 ....26 C2
Hester Cl HTWN L38 ....40 A3
Heversham SKEL WN8 ....33 H3
Heydon Cl FMBY L37 ....28 D5
Heyes Rd
 WGNW/BIL/OR WN5 ....39 H2
Heysham Rd CHTN/BK PR9 ....10 B3
Heywood Cl FMBY L37 ....29 E3
Higgin's La BRSC L40 ....22 D3
Higher La SKEL WN8 ....39 F1
Higher Vw SKEL WN8 ....39 F1
Highfield La BRSC L40 ....21 G1
Highfield Rd CHTN/BK PR9 ....5 H4
 ORM L39 ....26 D4
Highgate Rd SKEL WN8 ....39 E1
High La BRSC L40 ....27 F2
 ORM L39 ....31 H5
Highmeadow SKEL WN8 ....38 D2
High Moss ORM L39 ....30 D2
High Park Pl CHTN/BK PR9 ....10 C2
High Park Rd CHTN/BK PR9 ....10 C2
High St SKEL WN8 ....32 C5
Hilbre Cl CHTN/BK PR9 ....10 A1
Hillcrest SKEL WN8 ....37 C1
Hillcrest Dr BRSC L40 ....15 H5
Hillcrest Rd ORM L39 ....26 D4
Hilldean SKEL WN8 ....35 F5
Hillock Cl BRSC L40 ....21 E1
Hillock La BRSC L40 ....21 E1
Hillside Av ORM L39 ....30 C1
Hillside Rd STHP PR8 ....12 C4
Hill St CHTN/BK PR9 ....3 H2
Hillsview Rd STHP PR8 ....19 E4
Hilltop Wk ORM L39 ....30 B2
Hodge St STHP PR8 ....3 H3
Hodson St STHP PR8 ....3 K5
Hoghton Gv CHTN/BK PR9 ....3 J2
Hoghton St CHTN/BK PR9 ....3 H3
Holborn Dr ORM L39 ....30 B2
Holborn Hl ORM L39 ....30 B2
Holgate Dr
 WGNW/BIL/OR WN5 ....39 H3
Holland Moss SKEL WN8 ....37 F3
Hollybrook Rd STHP PR8 ....2 E7
Holly Cl SKEL WN8 ....32 D4
Holly Fold La ORM L39 ....36 D5
Holly La ORM L39 ....30 A1
 ORM L39 ....36 C4
Holmdale CHTN/BK PR9 ....6 A3
Holmfield Pk FMBY L37 ....28 D2
Holmwood Cl FMBY L37 ....28 D2
Holmwood Dr FMBY L37 ....28 D2
Holmwood Gdns FMBY L37 ....28 D2
Holt St
 WGNW/BIL/OR WN5 ....39 G3
Hoole La CHTN/BK PR9 ....7 E1
Hope Island SKEL WN8 ....33 E5
Hope Sq CHTN/BK PR9 ....3 K3
Hope St CHTN/BK PR9 ....3 K3
Hornby Rd CHTN/BK PR9 ....9 H3
Houghton's La SKEL WN8 ....33 H4
Houghtons Rd SKEL WN8 ....33 F2
Hulme St STHP PR8 ....3 H1
Huntingdon Ct
 CHTN/BK PR9 * 5 G5
Hurlston Av SKEL WN8 * 33 H5
Hurlston Dr ORM L39 ....33 H5
Hurlston La BRSC L40 ....26 A1
Hutton Ct SKEL WN8 ....32 C4
Hutton Rd SKEL WN8 ....32 C4
Hutton Wy ORM L39 ....26 D5
Hythe Cl STHP PR8 ....14 A2

I

Ilkley Av CHTN/BK PR9 ....6 A1
Ince Crs FMBY L37 ....28 D3
Inchfield SKEL WN8 ....33 G3
Inglesby Cnr BRSC L40 ....21 F4
Ingleton Rd STHP PR8 ....14 A2
Inglewhite SKEL WN8 ....33 F3
Ingram SKEL WN8 ....33 G4
Inskip SKEL WN8 ....33 H3
Inskip Rd CHTN/BK PR9 ....5 G3
Irton Rd CHTN/BK PR9 ....10 A2
Irvin Av CHTN/BK PR9 ....6 A2
Irving St STHP PR8 ....9 F1
Irwell SKEL WN8 ....33 F1
Ivybridge SKEL WN8 ....33 G3
Ivy Cl BRSC L40 ....23 H4
Ivydale SKEL WN8 ....33 G3
Ivy St STHP PR8 ....9 H4

J

Jacksmere La *BRSC* L40 .... **14** D5
Jane's Brook Rd *STHP* PR8 ...... **13** H1
Jubilee Av *ORM* L39 .... **27** E4
   WGNW/BIL/OR WN5 ... **39** G4
Jubilee Dr *SKEL* WN8 .... **32** D5
Jubilee Rd *FMBY* L37 .... **28** D5
Junction La *BRSC* L40 .... **23** F3

K

Keats Ter *STHP* PR8 .... **10** B4
Kempton Park Fold *STHP* PR8 .... **14** B2
Kendal Wy *STHP* PR8 .... **18** D5
Kenilworth Rd *STHP* PR8 .... **19** E4
Kensington Rd *CHTN/BK* PR9 ..... **3** K4
   FMBY L37 .... **29** E5
Kent Av *FMBY* L37 .... **29** G5
Kenton Cl *FMBY* L37 .... **24** B5
Kent Rd *FMBY* L37 .... **29** G5
   STHP PR8 .... **25** E1
Kenworthys Flats *CHTN/BK* PR9 ... **3** G2
Kenyons La *STHP* PR8 .... **19** E5
Kerfoot's La *SKEL* WN8 .... **32** B5
Kerslake Wy *HTWN* L38 .... **40** A3
Kerton Rw *STHP* PR8 * **12** D1
Kestral Pk *SKEL* WN8 .... **33** H1
Kestrel Ct *CHTN/BK* PR9 .... **9** H3
Kestrel Ms *SKEL* WN8 .... **33** H1
Keswick Cl *STHP* PR8 .... **19** E5
Kettering Rd *STHP* PR8 .... **18** D3
Kew House Dr *STHP* PR8 .... **14** C3
Kew Rd *FMBY* L37 .... **28** D5
   STHP PR8 .... **13** E2
Kilburn Rd *WGNW/BIL/OR* WN5 ... **39** F3
Killingbeck Cl *BRSC* L40 .... **14** C4
Kiln La *SKEL* WN8 .... **32** D3
Kingfisher Ct *CHTN/BK* PR9 ...... **9** H2
Kingfisher Pk *SKEL* WN8 .... **33** H1
Kingsbury Cl *STHP* PR8 .... **18** C4
Kingsbury Ct *SKEL* WN8 .... **33** H1
Kings Cl *FMBY* L37 .... **29** E4
Kings Hey Dr *CHTN/BK* PR9 ...... **10** B1
Kings Meadow *STHP* PR8 .... **19** F5
Kings Rd *FMBY* L37 .... **29** E4
Kingston Crs *CHTN/BK* PR9 .... **6** A2
King St *STHP* PR8 .... **3** F5
Kingsway *STHP* PR8 .... **2** E4
Kingswood Pk *STHP* PR8 .... **2** C6
Kinloch Wy *ORM* L39 .... **26** C5
Kirkdale Gdns *SKEL* WN8 * **38** C1
Kirkham Rd *CHTN/BK* PR9 .... **5** C3
Kirklake Bank *FMBY* L37 .... **28** C4
Kirklake Rd *FMBY* L37 .... **28** C4
Kirklees Rd *STHP* PR8 .... **12** D4
Kirkstall Dr *FMBY* L37 .... **29** H4
Kirkstall Rd *STHP* PR8 .... **12** D3
Knob Hall Gdns *CHTN/BK* PR9 .... **5** F4
Knob Hall La *CHTN/BK* PR9 ...... **5** F4
Knowle Av *STHP* PR8 .... **19** E2
Knowsley Ms *ORM* L39 .... **27** E5
Knowsley Rd *CHTN/BK* PR9 .... **9** F1
   ORM L39 .... **27** E5

L

Laburnum Dr *SKEL* WN8 .... **32** C4
Laburnum Gv *BRSC* L40 .... **23** C1
   STHP PR8 .... **10** B3
Lady Green La *HTWN* L38 * **41** F4
Lady Green La *HTWN* L38 .... **41** E4
Lady's Wk *BRSC* L40 .... **27** C5
Lafford La *SKEL* WN8 .... **35** F2
Lakes Dr *WGNW/BIL/OR* WN5 ..... **39** H5
Lakeside Av *WGNW/BIL/OR* WN5 .. **39** H5
Lakeside Ct *STHP* PR8 * **3** G2
Lambourne *SKEL* WN8 .... **33** G1
Lancaster Cl *STHP* PR8 .... **12** C1
Lancaster Crs *SKEL* WN8 .... **32** D4
Lancaster Dr *CHTN/BK* PR9 ...... **6** C3
Lancaster Ga *CHTN/BK* PR9 ...... **6** D2
Lancaster Rd *FMBY* L37 .... **29** E5
   STHP PR8 .... **12** C1
Land La *CHTN/BK* PR9 .... **6** A3
Langdale Av *FMBY* L37 .... **28** D3
Langdale Cl *FMBY* L37 .... **28** D4
Langdale Dr *BRSC* L40 .... **23** C4
Langdale Gdns *STHP* PR8 .... **12** D4
Langley *HTWN* L38 .... **40** A5
Langley Pl *BRSC* L40 .... **22** C3
Langley Rd *BRSC* L40 .... **22** C3
Langtree *SKEL* WN8 .... **33** G1

Lansdowne Rd *STHP* PR8 .... **10** A4
Larch Cl *SKEL* WN8 .... **32** D4
Larch St *STHP* PR8 .... **10** A5
Larch Wy *FMBY* L37 .... **28** D2
Larkfield La *CHTN/BK* PR9 .... **5** G4
Larkhill *SKEL* WN8 .... **33** G1
Larkhill Gv *HTWN* L38 .... **40** A4
Larkhill *FMBY* L37 .... **28** C2
Larkspur Cl *STHP* PR8 .... **9** H4
Latham Av *ORM* L39 .... **27** F5
Lathom Cl *BRSC* L40 .... **23** F3
Lathom La *BRSC* L40 .... **27** H3
Lathom Rd *CHTN/BK* PR9 .... **9** G1
Laurel Av *BRSC* L40 .... **23** F1
Laurel Dr *SKEL* WN8 .... **32** D3
Laurel Gv *STHP* PR8 .... **10** A3
Lawns Av *WGNW/BIL/OR* WN5 .... **39** F3
The Lawns *CHTN/BK* PR9 .... **5** F5
Lawson St *CHTN/BK* PR9 .... **10** C3
Lea Crs *ORM* L39 .... **26** D3
Leamington Rd *STHP* PR8 .... **19** E3
Ledburn *SKEL* WN8 .... **33** G2
Leeswood *SKEL* WN8 .... **33** G3
Leicester St *CHTN/BK* PR9 .... **3** H1
Lendel *FMBY* L37 .... **29** E3
Lenton Av *FMBY* L37 .... **28** D2
Lesley Rd *STHP* PR8 .... **10** A3
Lethbridge Rd *STHP* PR8 .... **9** H5
Levens Cl *CHTN/BK* PR9 .... **7** E2
Lexton Dr *CHTN/BK* PR9 .... **5** H4
Leybourne Av *STHP* PR8 .... **19** H1
Leyland Cl *CHTN/BK* PR9 .... **6** C2
Leyland Rd *CHTN/BK* PR9 .... **9** G1
Leyland Wy *ORM* L39 .... **27** E5
Lifeboat Rd *FMBY* L37 .... **28** A5
Lighthorne Dr *STHP* PR8 .... **18** C4
Lighthouse La *FMBY* L37 .... **29** G5
Lilac Av *STHP* PR8 .... **25** F1
Lilac Gv *SKEL* WN8 .... **32** D4
Limefield Dr *SKEL* WN8 .... **38** B1
Lime Gv *SKEL* WN8 .... **32** D4
Lime St *STHP* PR8 .... **10** A4
Lime Tree Wy *FMBY* L37 .... **28** C4
Limont Rd *STHP* PR8 .... **19** F3
Linaker St *STHP* PR8 .... **3** H7
Lincoln Rd *STHP* PR8 .... **13** E4
Linden Av *WGNW/BIL/OR* WN5 ... **39** H2
Linden Gv *WGNW/BIL/OR* WN5 .. **39** H2
Lindens *SKEL* WN8 .... **33** G1
Lindholme *SKEL* WN8 .... **33** H2
Lindley Av *WGNW/BIL/OR* WN5 .. **39** F3
Lingdales *FMBY* L37 .... **24** D5
Links Av *CHTN/BK* PR9 .... **5** E5
Little Hey La *FMBY* L37 .... **29** H1
Little La *CHTN/BK* PR9 .... **10** D1
Liverpool Old Rd *FMBY* L37 ...... **25** E4
Liverpool Rd *FMBY* L37 .... **29** G4
   ORM L39 .... **30** A3
   SKEL WN8 .... **32** B5
   STHP PR8 .... **12** D5
   STHP PR8 .... **25** E1
Liverpool Rd North *BRSC* L40 .... **23** E3
Liverpool Rd South *BRSC* L40 .... **22** D5
Lodge Rd *WGNW/BIL/OR* WN5 ... **39** H4
London La *STHP* PR8 .... **13** H5
London Sq *STHP* PR8 .... **3** G3
London St *STHP* PR8 .... **3** H4
Longacre *CHTN/BK* PR9 .... **5** F4
Longcliffe Dr *STHP* PR8 .... **18** D4
Longfield *FMBY* L37 .... **29** H1
Longford Rd *STHP* PR8 .... **13** E3
Longhey *SKEL* WN8 .... **33** H1
Long Heys La *SKEL* WN8 .... **34** B1
Long La *CHTN/BK* PR9 .... **7** F1
   ORM L39 .... **30** B2
   SKEL WN8 .... **38** B5
Long Meanygate *CHTN/BK* PR9 ... **11** H2
Longton Dr *FMBY* L37 .... **24** C5
Lonmore *CHTN/BK* PR9 .... **7** E2
Lonsdale Av *ORM* L39 .... **27** E3
Lonsdale Rd *FMBY* L37 .... **29** E3
   STHP PR8 .... **13** H1
Lordsgate Dr *BRSC* L40 .... **23** F4
Lordsgate La *BRSC* L40 .... **22** C5
Lord St *BRSC* L40 .... **23** F2
   STHP PR8 .... **2** D5
Lord St West *STHP* PR8 .... **2** E6
Lowcroft *SKEL* WN8 .... **33** H2
Lower Alt Rd *HTWN* L38 .... **40** A3
Lower Prom *STHP* PR8 .... **2** A4
Lowes Gn *FMBY* L37 .... **29** H5
Lowwood *HTWN* L38 .... **40** A1
Loxley Rd *STHP* PR8 .... **13** H1
Ludlow *SKEL* WN8 .... **33** H1
Ludlow Dr *ORM* L39 .... **26** C5
Lulworth *SKEL* WN8 .... **33** H1
Lulworth Rd *STHP* PR8 .... **12** D1
Lynbridge Cl
   WGNW/BIL/OR WN5 .... **39** H3

Lyndale *SKEL* WN8 .... **33** G1
Lyndhurst *SKEL* WN8 .... **33** G1
Lyndhurst Rd *STHP* PR8 .... **13** G3
Lynton Dr *STHP* PR8 .... **12** C4
Lynton Rd *STHP* PR8 .... **12** C5
Lynwood Av *ORM* L39 .... **30** B2
Lynwood Cl *SKEL* WN8 .... **38** A1
Lynwood End *ORM* L39 * **30** B2
Lyons Rd *STHP* PR8 .... **9** E5
Lytham Rd *CHTN/BK* PR9 .... **5** G3
Lytles Cl *FMBY* L37 .... **29** G2

M

Madingley Ct *CHTN/BK* PR9 * **5** F5
Maesbrook Cl *CHTN/BK* PR9 ..... **7** E2
Maiden Cl *SKEL* WN8 .... **32** B3
Malham Cl *STHP* PR8 .... **14** A2
Mallard Cl *ORM* L39 .... **30** B3
The Mallards *CHTN/BK* PR9 ..... **6** A4
Mallee Av *CHTN/BK* PR9 .... **5** G4
Mallee Crs *CHTN/BK* PR9 .... **5** G4
Maltkiln La *ORM* L39 .... **30** D5
Manchester Rd *CHTN/BK* PR9 .... **3** J2
Mandeville Rd *STHP* PR8 .... **18** D3
Manning Rd *SKEL* WN8 .... **33** F2
Manning Rd *STHP* PR8 .... **10** A4
Manor Av *BRSC* L40 .... **23** E5
Manor Crs *BRSC* L40 .... **23** E5
Manor Dr *BRSC* L40 .... **23** E5
Manor Gdns *BRSC* L40 .... **23** E5
Manor Gv *SKEL* WN8 .... **33** E4
Manor House Dr *SKEL* WN8 ..... **38** B5
Manor Ldg *FMBY* L37 .... **29** E2
Manor Rd *BRSC* L40 .... **23** E5
   CHTN/BK PR9 .... **5** C5
Manx Jane's La *CHTN/BK* PR9 ... **5** G3
Maple Av *BRSC* L40 .... **23** F3
Maple Cl *FMBY* L37 .... **28** C5
Maple St *STHP* PR8 .... **9** H4
Maplewood *SKEL* WN8 .... **33** F1
Marchbank Rd *SKEL* WN8 .... **32** C4
Mardale *STHP* PR8 .... **18** D4
Marians Dr *ORM* L39 .... **26** C2
Marina Rd *FMBY* L37 .... **29** F5
Marine Dr *CHTN/BK* PR9 ...... **4** B5
   STHP PR8 .... **2** A6
Marine Gate Man *CHTN/BK* PR9 * .. **3** H1
Marine Pde *STHP* PR8 .... **2** E1
Market St *STHP* PR8 .... **3** F4
Market Wy *ORM* L39 .... **26** D5
Markham Dr *STHP* PR8 .... **14** A3
Mark Rd *HTWN* L38 .... **40** A3
Marland *SKEL* WN8 .... **33** F1
Marlborough *SKEL* WN8 .... **33** F1
Marlborough Rd *CHTN/BK* PR9 ... **3** K3
Marl Gv *WGNW/BIL/OR* WN5 ... **39** G4
Marsden Rd *CHTN/BK* PR9 ..... **10** A3
Marshallsay *FMBY* L37 .... **29** G4
Marsh Brows *FMBY* L37 .... **29** E4
Marsh La *HTWN* L38 .... **41** E3
Marshside Rd
   CHTN/BK PR9 .... **5** E2
Marston Crs *HTWN* L38 .... **40** B3
Martin La *BRSC* L40 .... **17** E5
Martins La *SKEL* WN8 .... **38** A1
Mart La *BRSC* L40 .... **23** F2
Mary Av *STHP* PR8 .... **18** C5
Massam's La *FMBY* L37 .... **24** A5
Matlock Crs *STHP* PR8 .... **13** F2
Matlock Rd *STHP* PR8 .... **13** F2
Mawdsley Cl *FMBY* L37 .... **29** H3
Mawdsley Ter *ORM* L39 .... **27** E2
Maybank Cl
   CHTN/BK PR9 .... **10** C1
Mayfair Cl *HTWN* L38 .... **40** A5
Mayfield Av *FMBY* L37 .... **28** C5
Mayfield Cl *FMBY* L37 .... **28** C5
Mayfield Rd *SKEL* WN8 .... **38** D1
Maytree Wk *SKEL* WN8 .... **33** C1
Meadow Av *STHP* PR8 .... **13** G1
Meadow Bank *ORM* L39 * **27** E5
Meadowbrook *BRSC* L40 .... **23** E5
Meadow Brow
   CHTN/BK PR9 .... **6** B2
Meadow Cl *SKEL* WN8 .... **38** A1
Meadow Clough *SKEL* WN8 ..... **33** G1
Meadowcroft *FMBY* L37 .... **29** F4
   SKEL WN8 .... **33** G1
Meadow Dr *ORM* L39 .... **30** B3
Meadowfield *SKEL* WN8 .... **33** H1
Meadow La *STHP* PR8 .... **19** E5
The Meadows *STHP* PR8 * **19** F4
Meadow Vw *STHP* PR8 .... **13** H1
Meadway *SKEL* WN8 .... **33** F1
Melbreck *SKEL* WN8 .... **33** F1
Meldreth Cl *FMBY* L37 .... **28** C5

Melford Dr
   WGNW/BIL/OR WN5 .... **39**
Melling Rd *CHTN/BK* PR9 ...... **10**
Mellors Cl *STHP* PR8 .... **10**
Melrose Av *CHTN/BK* PR9 ...... **5**
Menivale Cl *CHTN/BK* PR9 ..... **5**
Meols Cl *FMBY* L37 .... **29**
Meols Cop Rd *STHP* PR8 .... **10**
Mercury Wy *SKEL* WN8 .... **34**
Mere Av *BRSC* L40 .... **23**
Mere Cl *SKEL* WN8 .... **33**
Mereland Cl *WGNW/BIL/OR* WN5 . **39**
Mere La *CHTN/BK* PR9 .... **7**
Merepark Dr *CHTN/BK* PR9 ..... **5**
Mere Rd *FMBY* L37 .... **28**
Meres Wy *STHP* PR8 .... **13**
Merewood *SKEL* WN8 .... **33**
Meriden Cl *STHP* PR8 .... **18**
Merlewood Av *CHTN/BK* PR9 ... **5**
Merscar La *BRSC* L40 .... **21**
Mersey Av *STHP* PR8 .... **24**
The Mews *STHP* PR8 .... **3**
Michaels Cl *FMBY* L37 .... **29**
Mickleton Dr *STHP* PR8 .... **18**
Middlecot Cl
   WGNW/BIL/OR WN5 .... **39**
Middlewood *SKEL* WN8 .... **33**
Midge Hall La *CHTN/BK* PR9 ... **16**
Midhurst Dr *STHP* PR8 .... **18**
Milford Cl *FMBY* L37 .... **28**
Millar's Pace *CHTN/BK* PR9 .... **5**
Millbank Brow *BRSC* L40 ...... **23**
Millbrook Cl *SKEL* WN8 .... **32**
Millcroft Av *WGNW/BIL/OR* WN5 . **39**
Mill Dam Cl *BRSC* L40 .... **22**
Mill Dam La *BRSC* L40 .... **22**
Millers Ct *ORM* L39 .... **27**
Millers Nook *SKEL* WN8 .... **35**
Millgreen Cl *SKEL* WN8 .... **33**
Mill House Vw *SKEL* WN8 ..... **39**
Millionaire Rw *BRSC* L40 ...... **21**
Mill La *BRSC* L40 .... **23**
   CHTN/BK PR9 .... **10**
   SKEL WN8 .... **33**
Mill Rd *STHP* PR8 .... **9**
   WGNW/BIL/OR WN5 .... **39**
Mill St *ORM* L39 .... **3**
   STHP PR8 .... **3**
Milman Cl *ORM* L39 .... **31**
Milton Dr *ORM* L39 .... **31**
Milton St *CHTN/BK* PR9 ...... **3**
Monks Carr La *HTWN* L38 ..... **41**
Monks Ct *FMBY* L37 .... **29**
Monks Dr *FMBY* L37 .... **29**
Montagu Rd *FMBY* L37 .... **29**
Montgomery Av *CHTN/BK* PR9 .. **10**
Montrose Dr *CHTN/BK* PR9 .... **10**
Moor Cl *STHP* PR8 .... **25**
Moor Dr *SKEL* WN8 .... **33**
Moorfield La *BRSC* L40 .... **21**
Moorgate *ORM* L39 .... **30**
Moorhouses *HTWN* L38 .... **40**
Moor La *HTWN* L38 .... **41**
   STHP PR8 .... **25**
Moor Rd
   WGNW/BIL/OR WN5 .... **39**
Morley Rd *CHTN/BK* PR9 ...... **10**
Mornington Rd
   CHTN/BK PR9 .... **3**
Morris La *ORM* L39 .... **20**
Morris Rd *SKEL* WN8 .... **38**
Morven Gv *STHP* PR8 .... **13**
Mosley St *STHP* PR8 .... **13**
Moss Av *WGNW/BIL/OR* WN5 ... **39**
Moss Bank *ORM* L39 .... **30**
Moss Delph La *ORM* L39 ...... **30**
Moss Gdns *STHP* PR8 .... **13**
Mossgiel Av *STHP* PR8 .... **13**
Moss La *BRSC* L40 .... **23**
   CHTN/BK PR9 .... **10**
   CHTN/BK PR9 .... **10**
   HTWN L38 .... **37**
   SKEL WN8 .... **37**
Moss Lane Vw *SKEL* WN8 ..... **37**
Moss Nook *BRSC* L40 .... **23**
   ORM L39 * **30**
Moss Rd *STHP* PR8 .... **13**
   WGNW/BIL/OR WN5 .... **39**
Moss Side *FMBY* L37 .... **29**
Motherwell Crs *STHP* PR8 ..... **14**
Mount House Cl *FMBY* L37 .... **29**
Mount House Rd *FMBY* L37 .... **29**
Mount St *CHTN/BK* PR9 .... **9**
The Mount *SKEL* WN8 * **33**
Mountwood *SKEL* WN8 .... **33**
Muirfield Dr *STHP* PR8 .... **18**
Mullion Cl *CHTN/BK* PR9 ..... **5**
Munro Av *WGNW/BIL/OR* WN5 .. **39**
Myrtle Gv *STHP* PR8 .... **10**

...aburn Dr WGNW/BIL/OR WN5 ....39 H3
...apier Ter STHP PR8 ....9 E5
...arrow Croft Rd ORM L39 ....30 A4
...arrow La ORM L39 ....30 A4
...eales Fold CHTN/BK PR9 ....6 B2
...elson St STHP PR8 ....12 D1
...elson St STHP PR8 ....3 F5
...everstitch Cl SKEL WN8 * 33 E3
...everstitch Rd SKEL WN8 ....32 C3
...evill St CHTN/BK PR9 ....3 C2
...ewby Cl STHP PR8 ....18 D5
...ew Court Wy ORM L39 ....27 E4
...ew Cut Cl STHP PR8 ....13 E5
...ew Cut La STHP PR8 ....13 E5
...ew Fold WGNW/BIL/OR WN5 ....39 F4
...ew Foul La CHTN/BK PR9 ....14 B1
...ew Hall Dr STHP PR8 ....9 C5
...ewgate Rd SKEL WN8 ....38 C1
...ewlands Av BRSC L40 ....23 G3
...ew La BRSC L40 ....22 C1
 ORM L39 ....11 H1
 ORM L39 ....30 D3
...ewlyn Dr SKEL WN8 ....38 A1
...ew Rd FMBY L37 ....29 C1
...ewton St CHTN/BK PR9 ....10 C3
...pe La RNFD/HAY WA11 ....37 E4
 SKEL WN8 ....37 C3
...xons La SKEL WN8 ....38 A1
 STHP PR8 ....19 C1
...el Ga ORM L39 ....30 A4
...olan St STHP PR8 ....9 C5
...orburn Crs FMBY L37 ....29 F4
...orbury Cl CHTN/BK PR9 ....6 A2
...orfolk Gv STHP PR8 ....12 D4
...orfolk Rd STHP PR8 ....12 D4
...ormanhurst ORM L39 ....31 F5
...orris House Dr ORM L39 ....30 B5
...orris Wy FMBY L37 ....29 H3
...ortham Ct CHTN/BK PR9 ....5 C2
...orth Dunes HTWN L38 ....40 A4
...orth End La HTWN L38 ....40 B2
...orthfield SKEL WN8 ....33 G1
...orth Leach Dr STHP PR8 ....18 C3
...orth Moss La FMBY L37 ....25 F4
...orth Rd CHTN/BK PR9 ....5 H3
...orth St CHTN/BK PR9 ....3 J1
...orthway ORM L39 ....30 A4
 SKEL WN8 ....33 G3
...orwood Av CHTN/BK PR9 ....10 A2
...orwood Crs CHTN/BK PR9 ....10 A2
...orwood Rd STHP PR8 ....18 C3
...e Nurseries FMBY L37 ....29 G4
...ursery La ORM L39 ....27 F4
...ursery Dr FMBY L37 ....29 F4
...uthall Rd STHP PR8 ....14 A2

...ak Av ORM L39 ....30 C1
...ak Crs SKEL WN8 ....32 C4
...ak Dr BRSC L40 ....23 G4
...akfield Dr FMBY L37 ....28 D2
...akfield Rd HTWN L38 ....40 A5
...akfields ORM L39 ....30 C1
...akford Cl CHTN/BK PR9 ....7 F2
...ak Gn ORM L39 ....29 E5
...akham Ct CHTN/BK PR9 * 3 K2
...ak St STHP PR8 ....10 A4
...akwood SKEL WN8 * 34 A2
...ak Tree Ct SKEL WN8 ....34 A2
...akwood Av STHP PR8 ....19 F2
...akwood Dr STHP PR8 ....19 C3
...ff Botanic Rd CHTN/BK PR9 ......10 C1
...d Acre HTWN L38 ....40 A4
...d Boundary Wy ORM L39 ....27 E4
...d Engine La SKEL WN8 ....32 B3
...d La FMBY L37 ....24 B5
...d Links CHTN/BK PR9 ....10 D2
...d Mill Hl ORM L39 ....30 C2
...d Mill La FMBY L37 ....29 F2
...d Park La ORM L39 ....10 C2
...d Town Cl SKEL WN8 ....32 C5
...d Town La FMBY L37 ....29 E2
...d Town Wy SKEL WN8 ....32 C5
 STHP PR8 ....10 A3
...nslow Crs STHP PR8 ....13 E3
...rchard WGNW/BIL/OR WN5 ...39 G5
...rchard La STHP PR8 ....19 F4
...e Orchards
 WGNW/BIL/OR WN5 ....39 H3
...e Orchard ORM L39 ....26 C5
...rchard Vw ORM L39 ....30 C4

Orchid Cl SKEL WN8 ....39 E2
Ormskirk Rd ORM L39 ....31 H4
 SKEL WN8 ....32 B4
Orms Wy FMBY L37 ....29 E3
Orrell Hill La HTWN L38 ....40 D3
Orrell La BRSC L40 ....23 E2
Orrell Ms BRSC L40 * 23 F2
Orrell Rd WGNW/BIL/OR WN5 ...39 H1
Orwell Cl STHP PR8 ....28 D5
Osborne Rd FMBY L37 ....18 D2
 STHP PR8 ....18 D2
Ottery Cl CHTN/BK PR9 ....5 G2
Ovington Dr STHP PR8 ....14 A2
Owen Av ORM L39 ....30 B2
Oxford Ct STHP PR8 ....12 D1
Oxford Gdns STHP PR8 ....12 C1
Oxford St SKEL WN8 ....32 D4
 STHP PR8 ....12 C1
Oxhouse Rd
 WGNW/BIL/OR WN5 ....39 F4

Paddock Rd SKEL WN8 ....37 H3
The Paddock FMBY L37 ....29 C1
 ORM L39 ....30 B2
 STHP PR8 ....18 D4
Padstow Cl CHTN/BK PR9 ....5 C2
Page Ct FMBY L37 ....29 F3
Palace Rd STHP PR8 ....2 C7
Palatine Rd STHP PR8 ....2 C7
Palm Ct SKEL WN8 ....32 B4
Palmerston Rd CHTN/BK PR9 .....10 B4
Palm Gv STHP PR8 ....12 C2
Paradise La FMBY L37 ....29 C1
Parbold Cl BRSC L40 ....23 F4
Park Av CHTN/BK PR9 ....10 A1
 FMBY L37 ....29 C1
 ORM L39 ....26 D5
Park Crs CHTN/BK PR9 ....9 H1
Parker Crs ORM L39 ....27 E3
Parkfield Cl ORM L39 ....30 B2
Parklands ORM L39 ....30 A2
 SKEL WN8 ....34 A3
Park Link ORM L39 ....30 A4
Park Rd CHTN/BK PR9 ....9 H2
 FMBY L37 ....29 E5
 ORM L39 ....26 D5
Park Rd West STHP PR8 ....9 G1
Parkside Av SKEL WN8 ....32 C5
Park Wall Rd HTWN L38 ....41 G4
Park Wy FMBY L37 ....29 H5
Parliament St SKEL WN8 ....35 F5
Parr's La ORM L39 ....30 C5
Parsonage Brow SKEL WN8 ....34 C1
Parsonage Rd STHP PR8 ....38 D1
Parsonage Rd SKEL WN8 ....38 D1
Part St STHP PR8 ....3 F7
The Pastures CHTN/BK PR9 ....6 B2
Patterdale Cl STHP PR8 ....18 D5
Paul's La CHTN/BK PR9 ....5 F4
Paxton Pl SKEL WN8 ....37 H4
Peel Rd SKEL WN8 ....38 A3
Peel St STHP PR8 ....10 B4
Peet Av ORM L39 ....30 C1
Peet's La CHTN/BK PR9 ....10 C1
Pendle Cl SKEL WN8 ....38 A5
Pendle Dr ORM L39 ....27 F4
Pendle Rd SKEL WN8 ....38 A4
Penketh Pl SKEL WN8 ....37 H3
Pennine Pl SKEL WN8 ....37 C2
Pennington Av ORM L39 ....26 D4
Penrith Av STHP PR8 ....18 D5
Penrose Pl SKEL WN8 ....38 A4
Perch Pool La CHTN/BK PR9 ......15 H1
Pershore Gv STHP PR8 ....18 C4
Peters Av BRSC L40 ....23 F3
Petworth Rd STHP PR8 ....19 G2
Philip Dr STHP PR8 ....19 G2
Phillip's Cl FMBY L37 ....29 F4
Phillips La ORM L39 ....29 F4
Pickles Dr BRSC L40 ....23 E3
Piercefield Rd FMBY L37 ....29 F2
Pikelaw Pl SKEL WN8 ....37 H3
Pilkington Rd STHP PR8 ....9 H5
Pilling Cl CHTN/BK PR9 ....5 F2
Pilling Pl SKEL WN8 ....37 H3
Pimbo La SKEL WN8 ....38 A1
Pimbo Rd SKEL WN8 ....37 H3
Pine Av ORM L39 ....27 E3
Pine Cl SKEL WN8 ....33 E4
Pine Crest ORM L39 ....30 A3
Pine Dr ORM L39 ....27 E4
Pine Gv CHTN/BK PR9 ....9 C4
 ORM L39 ....27 E3
Pinewood SKEL WN8 ....34 A2
Pinewood Av FMBY L37 ....28 D5

Pinewood Cl FMBY L37 ....28 D4
 STHP PR8 ....15 E4
Pinewood Crs
 WGNW/BIL/OR WN5 ....39 H2
Pinfold La BRSC L40 ....20 D5
 STHP PR8 ....18 C5
Pinfold Pl SKEL WN8 ....38 A4
Pippin St BRSC L40 ....22 B5
Pit Hey Pl SKEL WN8 ....37 H3
Pitts House La CHTN/BK PR9 .....10 D2
Pitt St CHTN/BK PR9 ....10 B4
Plantation Rd BRSC L40 ....22 C3
Platts La BRSC L40 ....23 E5
Plex Moss La FMBY L37 ....25 F2
Pool Hey La CHTN/BK PR9 ....15 E1
 STHP PR8 ....14 D2
Poolside Wk CHTN/BK PR9 ....5 H3
Pool St CHTN/BK PR9 ....6 A3
Poplar Dr SKEL WN8 ....33 E4
The Poplars BRSC L40 ....23 F5
Poplar St STHP PR8 ....10 A4
Poppy La ORM L39 ....31 G4
Portland St STHP PR8 ....3 C4
Post Office Av CHTN/BK PR9 ....3 H3
Potter Pl SKEL WN8 ....38 A3
Poulton Rd CHTN/BK PR9 ....10 B3
Preesall Cl CHTN/BK PR9 ....5 F5
Prescot Gn ORM L39 ....30 C2
Prescott Rd SKEL WN8 ....38 B4
Prestbury Av STHP PR8 ....18 D3
Preston New Rd CHTN/BK PR9 .....5 G4
Preston Rd CHTN/BK PR9 ....10 A2
Priesthouse Cl FMBY L37 ....29 G3
Priesthouse La FMBY L37 ....29 G3
Primrose Cl CHTN/BK PR9 ....6 A1
 FMBY L37 ....29 H1
Prince Charles Gdns STHP PR8 .....8 D5
Princes Gdn STHP PR8 ....10 A3
Princes St STHP PR8 ....3 F5
Priorswood Pl SKEL WN8 ....38 C4
Priory Cl BRSC L40 ....23 E4
 FMBY L37 ....29 H4
Priory Gdns STHP PR8 ....12 D1
Priory Gra STHP PR8 ....13 E1
Priory Gv ORM L39 ....30 C1
Priory Ms STHP PR8 ....2 D5
Priory Nook SKEL WN8 ....39 F1
Priory Rd SKEL WN8 ....39 F1
Proctor Rd FMBY L37 ....28 C2
Promenade CHTN/BK PR9 ....9 F1
 STHP PR8 ....18 B2
 STHP PR8 ....3 F3
Prospect Pl SKEL WN8 ....38 C3

Quarry Dr ORM L39 ....30 B4
Quarry Mt ORM L39 ....27 F4
Queen Anne St STHP PR8 ....30 B4
Queens Av FMBY L37 ....29 E1
Queens Cft FMBY L37 ....28 D4
Queens Rd CHTN/BK PR9 ....3 K2
 FMBY L37 ....28 D4
 WGNW/BIL/OR WN5 ....39 F3
Queen St ORM L39 ....30 D1
Quinton St STHP PR8 ....18 C4

Rabbit La BRSC L40 ....22 A4
Radnor Dr CHTN/BK PR9 ....5 F4
Railway Ap ORM L39 ....27 E5
Railway Pth ORM L39 ....30 D1
Railway Rd SKEL WN8 ....32 C5
Railway St STHP PR8 ....3 G7
Railway Ter STHP PR8 ....3 F7
Rainford Rd ORM L39 ....36 B4
Ralph's Wife's La CHTN/BK PR9 ...6 B4
Ranelagh Dr STHP PR8 ....19 H1
Rathbone Rd HTWN L38 ....40 A3
Rathmore Crs CHTN/BK PR9 ....5 H4
Ravenhead Dr SKEL WN8 ....38 D1
Ravenhead Wy SKEL WN8 ....38 C2
Raven Meols La FMBY L37 ....29 E4
Ravenscroft FMBY L37 ....29 F4
Ravenscroft Av ORM L39 ....30 D1
The Ravens FMBY L37 ....29 F4
Rawlinson Ct CHTN/BK PR9 * 9 H2
Rawlinson Gv CHTN/BK PR9 ....10 A1
Rawlinson Rd CHTN/BK PR9 ....10 A1
Rectory Rd CHTN/BK PR9 ....10 B1
Red Barnes FMBY L37 ....24 B5
Redcar St STHP PR8 ....14 B2
Redcliffe Gdns ORM L39 ....30 D2
Red Fold ORM L39 ....30 B3

Redgate FMBY L37 ....29 C4
 ORM L39 ....26 C5
Redgate Dr FMBY L37 ....29 H4
Redhills Dr STHP PR8 ....14 B2
Red Sands ORM L39 ....30 C2
Redwood Dr STHP PR8 ....30 C1
The Reeds ORM L39 ....26 C4
Rees Pk BRSC L40 ....23 G4
Regency Gdns STHP PR8 ....12 C1
Regent Cl STHP PR8 ....12 D1
Regent Ms STHP PR8 ....12 D1
Regent Rd STHP PR8 ....12 C1
Regents Fld FMBY L37 * 28 D1
Renacres La ORM L39 ....20 A4
Renfrey Cl ORM L39 ....26 D2
Ribble Av CHTN/BK PR9 ....6 A3
Richmond Av BRSC L40 ....23 F4
Richmond Cl HTWN L38 ....40 A5
Richmond Ms BRSC L40 ....23 F4
Richmond Rd STHP PR8 ....12 D3
Ridge Cl CHTN/BK PR9 ....6 A2
The Ridings CHTN/BK PR9 ....5 G4
Riding St STHP PR8 ....3 C6
Rimmer Gn STHP PR8 ....15 F4
Rimmer's Av FMBY L37 ....24 A5
 STHP PR8 ....3 C6
Ringtail Ct BRSC L40 ....22 C3
Ringtail Pl BRSC L40 ....22 C4
Ringtail Rd BRSC L40 ....22 B3
Ripon Cl STHP PR8 ....14 B2
River Cl FMBY L37 ....29 H5
Rivermeade STHP PR8 ....13 H1
Riverside HTWN L38 ....40 A3
Rivers St WGNW/BIL/OR WN5 ...39 H2
Rivington Cl FMBY L37 ....13 E2
Rivington Dr BRSC L40 ....23 F4
 SKEL WN8 ....39 F1
Roby Ml SKEL WN8 ....35 E2
Roe La CHTN/BK PR9 ....10 A2
Roe Park Ms CHTN/BK PR9 ....9 H2
Romiley Dr SKEL WN8 ....33 G5
Romsey Av FMBY L37 ....29 H4
Rookery Rd CHTN/BK PR9 ....10 A1
Rosebay Cl FMBY L37 ....29 G3
Rosebery St CHTN/BK PR9 ....10 C4
Rosebowl Vw BRSC L40 ....21 F4
Rose Crs SKEL WN8 ....32 D4
 STHP PR8 ....25 E1
Rosecroft Cl ORM L39 ....26 D4
Rose Hl STHP PR8 ....9 H4
Rosehill Dr ORM L39 ....30 B3
Roselea Dr CHTN/BK PR9 ....6 A3
Rosemary La FMBY L37 ....29 E3
Rose Pth FMBY L37 ....29 G4
Rose Pl ORM L39 ....30 C3
Rostron Crs FMBY L37 ....29 E5
Rothley Av STHP PR8 ....18 C4
Rothwell Cl ORM L39 ....26 C5
Rothwell Dr ORM L39 ....30 A3
 STHP PR8 ....18 C3
Rotten Rw STHP PR8 ....2 B7
The Roundway HTWN L38 ....40 A4
Rowan Cl BRSC L40 ....23 C1
Rowan La SKEL WN8 ....33 G1
Royal Cl FMBY L37 ....29 G5
Royal Crs FMBY L37 ....29 G4
Royal Pk STHP PR8 ....12 C1
Royal Ter STHP PR8 ....3 F4
Ruddington Rd STHP PR8 ....14 A3
Ruff La ORM L39 ....31 F1
Rufford Dr CHTN/BK PR9 ....6 D2
Rufford Rd CHTN/BK PR9 ....6 A4
Russell Av CHTN/BK PR9 ....10 C3
Russell Rd CHTN/BK PR9 ....10 C3
Rutland Crs ORM L39 ....26 C5
Rutland Rd STHP PR8 ....9 H5
Ryburn Rd ORM L39 ....30 C1
Rydal Av FMBY L37 ....28 D4
Ryder Cl ORM L39 ....30 B3
Ryder Crs ORM L39 ....30 B4
 STHP PR8 ....12 C5
The Rydinge FMBY L37 ....24 C5
Ryeground La FMBY L37 ....29 C1
Rymers Gn FMBY L37 ....29 E2

Sagar Fold ORM L39 ....30 C5
St Andrew's Pl STHP PR8 ....3 C5
St Anne's Cl FMBY L37 ....24 B5
St Anne's Pth FMBY L37 ....24 B5
St Annes Rd CHTN/BK PR9 ....5 F3
 FMBY L37 ....24 B5
 ORM L39 ....30 C1
St Bedes Cl ORM L39 ....30 C2
St Clair Dr CHTN/BK PR9 ....9 H4
St Cuthbert's Rd CHTN/BK PR9 ....5 H5

St George's Pl CHTN/BK PR9 ....3 G3
St George's Rd FMBY L37 ....29 E2
  HTWN L38 ....40 A2
Saint Helens Rd ORM L39 ....31 E1
St Helens Rd ORM L39 ....27 E5
St James Cl BRSC L40 ....31 H2
St James' Rd
  WGNW/BIL/OR WN5 ....39 G3
St James St STHP PR8 ....3 H7
St Johns Ct STHP PR8 * 19 F4
St John's Rd STHP PR8 ....19 F4
St Luke's Church Rd FMBY L37...28 C4
St Luke's Dr FMBY L37 ....28 C4
  WGNW/BIL/OR WN5 ....39 G4
St Luke's Gv CHTN/BK PR9 ....10 A3
St Luke's Rd CHTN/BK PR9 ....9 H3
St Mary's Gdns STHP PR8 ....19 H1
St Michael's Cl CHTN/BK PR9.....5 F4
St Paul's Pas STHP PR8 ....2 E6
St Paul's Sq STHP PR8 ....2 E6
St Paul's St STHP PR8 ....2 E6
St Peter's Av FMBY L37 ....28 D2
St Peter's Cl FMBY L37 ....28 D2
St Peter's Rd STHP PR8 ....13 E2
St Stephen's Rd HTWN L38 ....40 A3
St Thomas's Ct SKEL WN8 ....39 F1
St Vincent's Wy STHP PR8 ....12 D1
Salcombe Dr CHTN/BK PR9 ....5 G2
Salford Rd STHP PR8 ....19 E3
Salisbury St CHTN/BK PR9 ....10 C4
Sallowfields
  WGNW/BIL/OR WN5 ....39 G3
Sally's La CHTN/BK PR9 ....5 G5
Salwick Cl CHTN/BK PR9 ....5 F2
Sambourn Fold STHP PR8 ....18 C3
Sandbrook Gdns
  WGNW/BIL/OR WN5 ....39 G3
Sandbrook Rd STHP PR8 ....19 E5
  WGNW/BIL/OR WN5 ....39 F3
Sandfield Pk ORM L39 ....30 C3
Sandheys Dr STHP PR8 ....10 B1
Sandhills HTWN L38 ....40 A4
Sandhurst Cl FMBY L37 ....28 C5
Sandilands Gv HTWN L38 ....40 A4
Sandon Rd STHP PR8 ....12 C4
Sandringham Ct CHTN/BK PR9....3 H2
Sandringham Rd FMBY L37 ....29 E5
  STHP PR8 ....19 E3
Sandy La HTWN L38 ....40 B4
  SKEL WN8 ....32 C4
  WGNW/BIL/OR WN5 ....39 G4
Sanfield Cl ORM L39 ....26 C4
Sangness Dr STHP PR8 ....14 A2
Sanvino Av STHP PR8 ....19 F3
Saunders St CHTN/BK PR9.........9 F1
Savon Hook FMBY L37 ....29 H5
Sawdon Av STHP PR8 ....14 A1
Saxon Rd STHP PR8 ....8 D5
Scaffold La HTWN L38 ....40 D1
Scarisbrick Av STHP PR8 ....3 F3
Scarisbrick New Rd STHP PR8 ...14 A1
  STHP PR8 ....3 J7
Scarisbrick St CHTN/BK PR9 ....3 H4
  ORM L39 ....26 D4
Scarth Hill La ORM L39 ....30 D3
Scarth Pk SKEL WN8 ....37 H1
School Av FMBY L37 ....29 F3
School Cl ORM L39 * 30 B4
  STHP PR8 ....13 F3
School House Gn ORM L39 ....27 E5
School House Gv BRSC L40 ....23 E2
School Houses SKEL WN8 * 33 G5
School La BRSC L40 ....23 C2
  FMBY L37 ....29 F3
  SKEL WN8 ....32 C4
School Rd HTWN L38 ....40 A3
Schwartzman Dr CHTN/BK PR9....7 E1
Scott Dr ORM L39 ....27 E3
Scott St CHTN/BK PR9 ....10 C3
Seabank Rd CHTN/BK PR9 ....3 H1
Seacroft Crs CHTN/BK PR9 ....5 F5
Seafield FMBY L37 ....29 G4
Seafield Rd STHP PR8 ....19 E2
Sealand Av FMBY L37 ....28 D4
Sealand Cl FMBY L37 ....28 D4
Seaton Pl SKEL WN8 ....32 D2
Seaton Wy CHTN/BK PR9 ....5 G2
Seddon Pl SKEL WN8 ....32 D2
Sefton Av WGNW/BIL/OR WN5 ...39 G3
Sefton Cl WGNW/BIL/OR WN5...39 G3
Sefton Rd FMBY L37 ....29 E4
  WGNW/BIL/OR WN5 ....39 G3
Sefton St STHP PR8 ....13 F1
  STHP PR8 ....3 J6
Sefton Vw WGNW/BIL/OR WN5...39 G3
Segar's La STHP PR8 ....19 F3
Selby Dr CHTN/BK PR9 ....29 H4
Selby Pl SKEL WN8 ....32 C4
Selworthy Rd STHP PR8 ....12 B2

Sephton Dr ORM L39 ....27 E3
The Serpentine ORM L39 ....30 C5
Sevenoaks Av STHP PR8 ....18 D3
Shaftesbury Av STHP PR8 ....13 E5
Shaftesbury Gv STHP PR8 ....13 E4
Shaftesbury Rd STHP PR8 ....13 E5
Shakespeare St STHP PR8 ....3 G7
Shaw Crs FMBY L37 ....29 H2
Shaw's Av STHP PR8 ....13 E4
Shaw's Rd STHP PR8 ....13 E4
Shelley Dr ORM L39 ....26 C4
Shelley Gv STHP PR8 ....10 B3
Shellfield Rd CHTN/BK PR9 ....5 G4
Shelton Dr STHP PR8 ....18 C4
Shenley Wy CHTN/BK PR9 * 6 B2
Sherrat St SKEL WN8 ....32 C4
Sherringham Rd STHP PR8 ....12 C3
Sherwood Av ORM L39 ....30 B3
Sherwood Dr SKEL WN8 ....34 A2
Shirdley Crs STHP PR8 ....19 E5
Shireburn Rd FMBY L37 ....28 C1
Shirewell Rd
  WGNW/BIL/OR WN5 ....39 H3
Shore Rd STHP PR8 ....18 B2
Sidney Rd CHTN/BK PR9 ....10 B2
Silverthorne Dr CHTN/BK PR9 ...10 B1
Skipton Av STHP PR8 ....6 A1
Slackey La CHTN/BK PR9 ....6 A3
Slaidburn Crs STHP PR8 ....5 G2
Slate La SKEL WN8 ....32 B3
Small La BRSC L40 ....17 E5
  ORM L39 ....31 E1
Smith St SKEL WN8 ....32 C4
Smithy Cl FMBY L37 ....29 H2
Smithy Glen Dr
  WGNW/BIL/OR WN5 ....39 H4
Smithy Gn FMBY L37 ....29 G2
Smithy La BRSC L40 ....21 G4
Snape Gn STHP PR8 ....15 F5
Snoballey BRSC L40 ....21 F4
Somerset Dr STHP PR8 ....25 E1
Southbank Rd STHP PR8 ....3 H7
Southern Rd STHP PR8 ....2 E6
Southport New Rd CHTN/BK PR9..7 F3
Southport Old Rd FMBY L37 .....24 D4
Southport Rd BRSC L40 ....20 B1
  BRSC L40 ....26 C2
  FMBY L37 ....29 C1
South Ter ORM L39 ....30 D1
Southway SKEL WN8 ....33 G5
Spa La BRSC L40 ....32 A1
Spencer Pl CHTN/BK PR9 * 3 K4
Spencers La SKEL WN8 ....33 G5
Spinney Cl ORM L39 ....30 C2
The Spinney FMBY L37 ....29 C1
Spring Cl STHP PR8 ....9 E5
Springfield Cl BRSC L40 ....23 E5
  FMBY L37 ....28 C4
Spruce Wy FMBY L37 ....28 C3
Spymers Cft FMBY L37 ....24 C5
Square House La STHP PR8 * 3 K4
Square La BRSC L40 ....23 F4
The Square BRSC L40 ....21 F4
Squirrel Gn FMBY L37 ....28 C1
Stafford Rd STHP PR8 ....13 E4
Stafford St SKEL WN8 ....32 C3
Stamford Rd STHP PR8 ....13 F2
Standhouse La ORM L39 ....30 B3
Standside Pk SKEL WN8 ....32 C5
Stanlawe Rd FMBY L37 ....24 A5
Stanley Av STHP PR8 ....12 D3
Stanley Ct BRSC L40 ....23 F2
Stanley Rd FMBY L37 ....24 A5
  SKEL WN8 ....38 D1
Stanley St CHTN/BK PR9 ....3 G3
  ORM L39 ....27 E5
Stanley Wy SKEL WN8 ....32 D2
Stannought Rd SKEL WN8 ....34 A2
Statham Rd BRSC L40 ....32 B1
Statham Wy ORM L39 ....30 D1
Station Ap BRSC L40 ....23 F2
  ORM L39 * 27 E5
Station Av WGNW/BIL/OR WN5...39 G3
Station Rd CHTN/BK PR9 ....6 D2
  ORM L39 ....27 E4
  STHP PR8 ....19 E3
Staveley Av BRSC L40 ....23 F3
Staveley Rd SKEL WN8 ....32 D2
  STHP PR8 ....19 F4
Stephenson Wy STHP PR8 ....29 H3
The Stiles ORM L39 ....26 D5
Stoneleigh Cl STHP PR8 ....19 E4
Stoney Brow SKEL WN8 ....35 E3
Storwood Cl
  WGNW/BIL/OR WN5 ....39 H3
Stourton Rd STHP PR8 ....19 E4
Straight Up La CHTN/BK PR9 .....11 E2
Stratford Cl STHP PR8 ....18 C2

Stretton Dr CHTN/BK PR9 ....10 B2
Stub La BRSC L40 ....22 B5
Sturgess Cl ORM L39 ....27 E3
Suffolk Rd STHP PR8 ....13 E5
Sugar Stubbs La CHTN/BK PR9...7 G5
Sulby Cl STHP PR8 ....12 D2
Summer St SKEL WN8 ....33 E1
Sumner Rd FMBY L37 ....29 F3
Sunbury Dr STHP PR8 ....18 D4
Sunningdale Gdns FMBY L37 ....29 E3
Sunnyfields ORM L39 ....27 F5
Sunny Rd CHTN/BK PR9 ....5 G5
Sunnyside STHP PR8 ....12 D2
Sussex Rd CHTN/BK PR9 ....3 K4
  STHP PR8 ....10 A4
Sutton Rd FMBY L37 ....29 F3
Swan Delph ORM L39 ....30 B3
Swanpool La ORM L39 ....30 B3
Swift's Fold SKEL WN8 ....32 C5
Sycamore Dr SKEL WN8 ....32 D3
Sycamore Gv FMBY L37 ....28 C5

T

Tadlow Cl FMBY L37 ....28 C5
Talaton Cl CHTN/BK PR9 ....5 G2
Talbot Dr STHP PR8 ....3 G5
Talbot St STHP PR8 ....3 F6
The Tamneys SKEL WN8 ....33 E4
Tanfields SKEL WN8 ....33 H5
Tanhouse Rd SKEL WN8 ....33 H5
Tarleswood SKEL WN8 ....33 H5
Tarleton Rd CHTN/BK PR9 ....10 C2
Tarlswood SKEL WN8 ....33 H4
Tarn Brow ORM L39 ....30 B2
Tarn Rd FMBY L37 ....28 D3
Tarnside Rd WGNW/BIL/OR WN5..39 H2
Tarvin Cl CHTN/BK PR9 ....6 B2
Tavistock Dr STHP PR8 ....18 D2
Tawd Rd SKEL WN8 ....33 H5
Taylor Av ORM L39 ....27 F5
Taylor St SKEL WN8 ....32 B4
Teal Cl ORM L39 ....30 B3
Tedder Av CHTN/BK PR9 ....10 C3
Tennyson Dr ORM L39 ....26 C4
Teversham SKEL WN8 ....33 E3
Tewkesbury SKEL WN8 * 32 D3
Thanet SKEL WN8 ....33 E3
Thealby Cl SKEL WN8 ....32 D3
Thirlmere Av FMBY L37 ....29 G4
  SKEL WN8 ....39 E1
Thirlmere Dr STHP PR8 ....18 D5
Thirlmere Ms HTWN L38 * 40 B3
Thirlmere Rd HTWN L38 ....40 B3
Thirsk SKEL WN8 ....32 D3
Thistleton Ms CHTN/BK PR9 .....3 K2
Thompson Av ORM L39 ....27 F5
Thornbeck Av HTWN L38 ....40 A4
Thornbridge Av BRSC L40 ....23 F4
Thornbury SKEL WN8 ....33 E3
Thornhill ORM L39 ....30 A4
Thornton Rd CHTN/BK PR9 ....10 B3
Thornwood SKEL WN8 ....33 E3
Thoroughgood Cl BRSC L40.......23 E5
Thorpe SKEL WN8 ....33 E3
Three Pools CHTN/BK PR9 ....6 A4
Three Tuns La FMBY L37 ....29 F3
Threlfalls La CHTN/BK PR9 ....5 F5
Thurcroft Dr SKEL WN8 ....32 D3
Thursby Cl STHP PR8 ....18 D5
Thurston Rd SKEL WN8 ....32 D3
Tilcroft SKEL WN8 ....32 D3
Timms Cl FMBY L37 ....29 F1
Timms La FMBY L37 ....29 F1
Tinsley Av STHP PR8 ....14 A2
Tinsley's La STHP PR8 ....14 B4
Tintagel SKEL WN8 ....32 C4
Tintern Dr FMBY L37 ....29 H4
Tithebarn Rd STHP PR8 ....9 H4
Tithebarn St SKEL WN8 * 39 E1
Tiverton Av SKEL WN8 ....32 D3
Todd's La CHTN/BK PR9 ....7 E1
Tollgate Crs BRSC L40 ....22 B4
Tollgate Rd BRSC L40 ....22 C5
Tongbarn SKEL WN8 ....32 D3
Tontine Rd SKEL WN8 ....39 F2
Top Acre Rd SKEL WN8 ....37 H1
Torcross Cl CHTN/BK PR9 ....5 G2
Totnes Dr CHTN/BK PR9 ....5 G2
Tourer Ter BRSC L40 ....21 F4
Tower Buildings CHTN/BK PR9 * ...3 J1
Tower End FMBY L37 ....28 C1
Tower Hl ORM L39 ....27 F5
Tower Hill Rd SKEL WN8 ....38 D3
Tower Nook SKEL WN8 ....38 D3
Town End Cl ORM L39 ....30 C1
Town Green La ORM L39 ....30 B5

Town La STHP PR8 13
Town Lane (Kew) STHP PR8 13
Tracks La WGNW/BIL/OR WN5 ...39
Trafalgar Rd STHP PR8 12
Trap Hl FMBY L37 28
Treen Cl CHTN/BK PR9 5
Treesdale Cl STHP PR8 12
Treetop Vls CHTN/BK PR9 * 5
Trent Cl BRSC L40 23
Trevor Rd BRSC L40 23
  STHP PR8 19
Trinity Gdns STHP PR8 3
Trinity Ms CHTN/BK PR9 3
Truro Av CHTN/BK PR9 3
Truscott Rd BRSC L40 23
Tudor Rd STHP PR8 18
Tulketh St STHP PR8 3
Turnacre FMBY L37 24
Turnberry SKEL WN8 32
Turnberry Wy CHTN/BK PR9 6
Turners Yd
  WGNW/BIL/OR WN5 * 39
Turning La STHP PR8 14
Twistfield Cl STHP PR8 2
Tyrer Rd ORM L39 27
Tyrers Cl FMBY L37 29

U

Uldale Cl STHP PR8 18
Union St CHTN/BK PR9 3
Unit Rd STHP PR8 19
Upholland Rd
  WGNW/BIL/OR WN5 39
Upper Aughton Rd STHP PR8 9
Uppingham SKEL WN8 32
Upton Av STHP PR8 18

V

Vale Crs STHP PR8 25
Vale Cft SKEL WN8 38
Varlian Cl BRSC L40 31
Vaughan Cl FMBY L37 28
Vaughan Rd STHP PR8 13
Vernon Rd CHTN/BK PR9 10
Verulam Rd CHTN/BK PR9 3
Vicarage Cl BRSC L40 31
  FMBY L37 28
Vicarage Gdns BRSC L40 23
Vicarage Rd FMBY L37 28
  WGNW/BIL/OR WN5 39
Vicarage Wk ORM L39 26
Victoria Bridge Rd STHP PR8 3
Victoria Ct STHP PR8 12
Victoria Pk SKEL WN8 32
Victoria Rd FMBY L37 13
  HTWN L38 41
  ORM L39 30
Victoria St BRSC L40 23
  CHTN/BK PR9 3
Victoria Wy FMBY L37 28
  STHP PR8 2
Victory Av CHTN/BK PR9 10
Viking Cl STHP PR8 18
Village Cl SKEL WN8 32
Village Wy HTWN L38 40
  SKEL WN8 32
Virginia St STHP PR8 13
Vivian Dr STHP PR8 13
Vulcan St CHTN/BK PR9 3

W

Walker Cl FMBY L37 29
The Walk STHP PR8 9
Wallcroft St SKEL WN8 32
Walmer Ct STHP PR8 12
Walmer Rd STHP PR8 13
Walnut St STHP PR8 13
Walro Ms CHTN/BK PR9 5
Walton St CHTN/BK PR9 3
Ward Av FMBY L37 28
Warpers Moss Cl BRSC L40 23
Warper's Moss La BRSC L40 23
Warren Ct STHP PR8 2
Warren Gn FMBY L37 28
Warren Rd CHTN/BK PR9 10
Warwick Cl STHP PR8 13
Warwick St STHP PR8 13
Washbrook Wy ORM L39 30
Watchyard La FMBY L37 29
Waterfoot Av STHP PR8 18

ater La CHTN/BK PR9 ....6 B2
aterloo Rd STHP PR8 ....12 C3
atermede
WGNW/BIL/OR WN5 ....39 H5
aterworks Rd ORM L39 ....27 F4
avell Av CHTN/BK PR9 ....10 D3
avell Cl CHTN/BK PR9 ....10 D3
averley SKEL WN8 ....32 C4
averley St STHP PR8 ....3 G3
ayfarers Ar STHP PR8 * 3 G3
eaver Av BRSC L40 ....23 G2
elbeck Rd STHP PR8 ....12 D1
elbeck Ter STHP PR8 ....12 D1
elbourne SKEL WN8 ....32 C4
eld Dr FMBY L37 ....28 D2
eldon Dr ORM L39 ....31 E1
eld Pde STHP PR8 ....12 D1
eld Rd STHP PR8 ....2 B7
ellcross Rd SKEL WN8 ....39 E2
ellfield La BRSC L40 ....31 H3
ellington Cl SKEL WN8 ....34 B5
ellington St STHP PR8 ....2 E5
elwyn Av STHP PR8 ....19 F2
ennington Rd CHTN/BK PR9 .....10 B4
entworth Cl STHP PR8 ....3 G5
escoe Cl WGNW/BIL/OR WN5 ....39 H3
esley St STHP PR8 ....3 G5
estbourne Gdns STHP PR8 ......12 C1
estbourne Rd STHP PR8 ....12 B1
estcliffe Rd STHP PR8 ....2 C7
esterdale Dr CHTN/BK PR9 ......7 F2
estgate SKEL WN8 ....32 C4
estgate Dr
WGNW/BIL/OR WN5 ....39 G3
esthaven Crs ORM L39 ....30 B5
esthill STHP PR8 * 2 E6
est La FMBY L37 ....24 B5
estminster Dr STHP PR8 ....18 C3
estmoreland Rd STHP PR8 ......9 G5
est Park Cl SKEL WN8 ....32 C5
est St STHP PR8 ....3 F4

Westway HTWN L38 ....40 A3
Westwood Cl STHP PR8 ....14 A2
Whalley Dr FMBY L37 ....29 G4
ORM L39 ....30 B5
Whalleys Rd SKEL WN8 ....33 G1
Wheatacre SKEL WN8 ....32 D5
Wheat La BRSC L40 ....23 H4
Wheelwrights Whf BRSC L40 .....20 D4
Whitby Av CHTN/BK PR9 ....5 H4
Whitefield Cl HTWN L38 ....40 A5
Whitehaven Cl STHP PR8 ....18 D5
Whitehey Rd SKEL WN8 ....32 D5
Whitehouse Av FMBY L37 ....29 G4
White House La BRSC L40 ....16 C4
Whitehouse La FMBY L37 ....29 G4
Whiteledge Rd SKEL WN8 ....33 G5
Whiteley's La BRSC L40 ....31 H3
White Moss La SKEL WN8 ....36 B1
White Moss Rd South
SKEL WN8 ....36 D1
Whiterails Dr ORM L39 ....26 C4
Whiterails Ms ORM L39 ....26 B4
Whitestock SKEL WN8 ....32 D5
Whitley Rd SKEL WN8 ....35 F2
Whitstone Dr SKEL WN8 ....38 A1
Whittle Dr ORM L39 ....26 D3
Wholesome La BRSC L40 ....16 C5
Wicks Crs FMBY L37 ....28 C2
Wicks Gdns FMBY L37 ....29 E3
Wicks Gn FMBY L37 ....28 C3
Wicks Green Cl FMBY L37 ....28 C2
Wicks La FMBY L37 ....28 C3
Wigan Rd ORM L39 ....27 E5
SKEL WN8 ....33 E5
Wight Moss Wy STHP PR8 ....13 H2
Wignalls Meadow HTWN L38 .....40 A4
Wigston Cl STHP PR8 ....18 D4
Wilcove SKEL WN8 ....33 E4
Willard Av WGNW/BIL/OR WN5 ...39 G5
Willow Crs BRSC L40 ....23 G1
Willow Dr SKEL WN8 ....32 D4

Willow End BRSC L40 ....23 G3
Willow Gn ORM L39 ....27 E5
Willow Gv FMBY L37 ....29 F2
STHP PR8 ....10 A3
Willowhey CHTN/BK PR9 ....5 F4
Willow Hey SKEL WN8 ....33 E4
The Willows STHP PR8 * 13 G1
Willow Wk SKEL WN8 ....33 G1
Wilmcote Gv CHTN/BK PR9 ......18 D4
Wilsham Rd
WGNW/BIL/OR WN5 ....39 H3
Wimbrick Cl ORM L39 ....30 C1
Wimbrick Crs ORM L39 ....30 C2
Windermere Crs STHP PR8 ....19 E5
Windermere Rd HTWN L38 ....40 B3
Windmill Av SKEL WN8 ....27 E5
Windmill Hts SKEL WN8 ....34 D5
Windrows SKEL WN8 ....33 E4
Windsor Cl BRSC L40 ....23 F4
Windsor Ct STHP PR8 ....12 C1
Windsor Rd CHTN/BK PR9 ....9 H4
FMBY L37 ....29 E5
SKEL WN8 ....34 D5
Windy Harbour Rd STHP PR8 ....19 G1
Winifred La ORM L39 ....30 A4
Winstanley Rd SKEL WN8 ....33 E5
The Winsters SKEL WN8 ....33 E4
Winston Crs STHP PR8 ....14 A3
Witham Rd SKEL WN8 ....32 C4
Withins Fld HTWN L38 ....40 A4
Wollaton Dr STHP PR8 ....14 B2
Wolverton SKEL WN8 ....33 E5
Woodcroft SKEL WN8 ....33 E5
Woodfield Rd ORM L39 ....30 B2
Woodland Av BRSC L40 ....20 D1
Woodlands Cl CHTN/BK PR9 ......9 H2
FMBY L37 ....28 D4
ORM L39 ....31 F1
Woodlands Rd FMBY L37 ....28 D4
The Woodlands BRSC L40 ....23 H4
STHP PR8 ....19 E3

Woodlea Cl CHTN/BK PR9 ....6 B2
Woodley Park Rd SKEL WN8 .....33 G1
Woodmoss La STHP PR8 ....15 G3
Woodrow SKEL WN8 ....32 D5
Woodside Av STHP PR8 ....18 D5
Woodside Cl SKEL WN8 ....35 F5
Woodstock Dr STHP PR8 ....12 D5
Woodvale Ct CHTN/BK PR9 ....7 E2
Woodvale Rd STHP PR8 ....25 E1
Wordsworth Cl ORM L39 ....26 C4
Worthing Cl STHP PR8 ....12 D2
Wrights Ter STHP PR8 ....13 F2
Wright St CHTN/BK PR9 ....3 H3
Wrigleys Cl FMBY L37 ....29 F1
Wrigleys La FMBY L37 ....29 F1
Wyke Cop Rd CHTN/BK PR9 .....15 F2
Wyke La CHTN/BK PR9 ....15 F1
Wyke Wood La CHTN/BK PR9 ....11 H2
Wyresdale Av STHP PR8 ....13 H1

Y

Yeadon SKEL WN8 ....33 G4
Yellow House La STHP PR8 ....3 G6
Yewdale SKEL WN8 ....33 F4
Yew Tree Rd ORM L39 ....27 E4
York Av STHP PR8 ....2 E7
York Cl FMBY L37 ....24 B5
York Gdns STHP PR8 ....9 E5
York Mnr FMBY L37 * 29 F3
York Rd FMBY L37 ....29 F3
STHP PR8 ....12 D1
York Ter CHTN/BK PR9 ....3 K2

Z

Zetland St CHTN/BK PR9 ....9 H3

Index - featured places

bey Farm Caravan Park
BRSC L40 ....27 H2
bey Lakes Sports Centre
WGNW/BIL/OR WN5 ....39 G1
bey Lane Industrial Estate
BRSC L40 ....27 H1
BC Cinema
STHP PR8 ....3 G4
nsdale CE Primary School
STHP PR8 ....19 F4
nsdale Clinic
STHP PR8 ....19 F5
nsdale Hope CE High School
STHP PR8 ....19 E2
nsdale Sand Dunes National
Nature Reserve
STHP PR8 ....24 A1
Business Park
CHTN/BK PR9 ....10 C4
den College
CHTN/BK PR9 ....3 J4
gyle Lawn Tennis Club
CHTN/BK PR9 ....5 E5
hurst Health Centre
SKEL WN8 ....33 G1
small Primary School
ORM L39 ....26 C3
kinson Art Gallery
STHP PR8 ....3 G4
tlanta Swimming
STHP PR8 ....13 E1
ughton Christ Church
Primary School
ORM L39 ....30 B2
ughton St Michaels CE
Primary School
ORM L39 ....30 A4
ughton Town Green
Primary School
ORM L39 ....30 B5
almoral Lodge Hotel
CHTN/BK PR9 ....3 K1
nks Health Centre
CHTN/BK PR9 ....6 D1
nks Methodist Primary School
CHTN/BK PR9 ....7 F1
eacon Country Park
SKEL WN8 ....34 C4
eacon Park Golf & Country Club
SKEL WN8 ....34 B3

Beacon School
SKEL WN8 ....34 B5
Best Western Royal Clifton
Hotel STHP PR8 ....3 F4
Best Western Stutelea Hotel
CHTN/BK PR9 ....9 G1
Birkdale Cemetery
STHP PR8 ....19 G1
Birkdale High School
STHP PR8 ....19 G1
Birkdale Primary School
STHP PR8 ....13 F2
Birkdale RC Cemetery
STHP PR8 ....19 G2
Birkdale Trading Estate
STHP PR8 ....12 D3
Birleywood Health Centre
SKEL WN8 ....38 A2
Bishop David Sheppard CE
Primary School
CHTN/BK PR9 ....10 D3
Bishop Martin CE Primary
School SKEL WN8 ....38 A1
Black Moss School
SKEL WN8 ....32 C3
Blowick Business Centre
CHTN/BK PR9 ....10 C4
Bold Hotel
CHTN/BK PR9 ....3 H2
Botanic Gardens Museum
CHTN/BK PR9 ....5 H5
The British Lawnmower
Museum
STHP PR8 ....3 G7
Brookfield Community
Primary School
SKEL WN8 ....32 C3
Burscough Bridge Methodist
Primary School
BRSC L40 ....23 E2
Burscough CC
BRSC L40 ....23 G3
Burscough Health Centre
BRSC L40 ....23 F2
Burscough Industrial Estate
BRSC L40 ....22 C2
Burscough Primary School
BRSC L40 ....23 G2
Burscough Priory Science College
BRSC L40 ....23 E2

Burscough Sports Centre
BRSC L40 ....23 F2
Cambridge House Hotel
CHTN/BK PR9 ....10 A1
Canning Road Industrial Estate
CHTN/BK PR9 ....10 C4
Carlton Lawn Tennis Club
STHP PR8 ....12 D3
Childrens Centre
ORM L39 ....31 F2
Christ the King Catholic
High School & Sixth Form
STHP PR8 ....13 F3
Churchtown Medical Centre
CHTN/BK PR9 ....5 G5
Churchtown Primary School
CHTN/BK PR9 ....5 H5
Clarence House School
FMBY L37 ....24 A5
Cobbs Brow Community
School SKEL WN8 ....33 F2
Concourse Shopping Centre
SKEL WN8 ....33 G4
Crawford Village
Primary School
SKEL WN8 ....38 B5
Crossens CC
CHTN/BK PR9 ....6 B3
Cross Hall High School Adult
Education Centre
ORM L39 ....27 G5
Crowland Street Industrial
Estate
CHTN/BK PR9 ....10 B4
Crow Orchard Primary School
SKEL WN8 ....33 E3
Dalweb Industrial Park
CHTN/BK PR9 ....7 G4
Dean Wood Golf Club
SKEL WN8 ....35 F5
Delph Side Primary School
SKEL WN8 ....33 G5
East Gillbrands Industrial
Estate SKEL WN8 ....37 F1
Edge Hill College of
Higher Education
ORM L39 ....31 F1
Edge Hill University
(Ormskirk Campus)
ORM L39 ....31 F2

Fairlie CP School
SKEL WN8 ....33 G2
Farnborough Road J & I School
STHP PR8 ....12 D5
Formby AFC
FMBY L37 ....29 F3
Formby CC
FMBY L37 ....29 F1
Formby Golf Club
FMBY L37 ....28 D1
Formby Hall Golf &
Country Club
FMBY L37 ....25 E3
Formby High School
FMBY L37 ....29 E2
Formby Junior Sports Club
FMBY L37 ....29 G1
Formby Ladies Golf Club
FMBY L37 ....28 D1
Formby Lawn Tennis Club
FMBY L37 ....29 F1
Freshfield Primary School
FMBY L37 ....29 G2
Freshlea Private Clinic
FMBY L37 ....28 D5
Funland
STHP PR8 ....3 F2
Fylde Road Industrial Estate
CHTN/BK PR9 ....5 H3
Glenburn Sports College
SKEL WN8 ....33 F5
Greenbank High School
STHP PR8 ....12 C4
Guys Industrial Estate
BRSC L40 ....22 C5
Hall Green Clinic
SKEL WN8 ....39 E1
Hesketh Centre (Hospital)
CHTN/BK PR9 ....9 G1
Hesketh Golf Club
CHTN/BK PR9 ....5 E5
Hewitt Business Park
WGNW/BIL/OR WN5 ....39 H4
Hillside Community
Primary School
SKEL WN8 ....34 A5
Hillside Golf Club
STHP PR8 ....12 C4
Hillside Health Centre
SKEL WN8 ....33 H4

Holland Business Park
  BRSC L40 ....**32** B1
Holland Moor Primary School
  SKEL WN8 ....**38** B1
Holy Family Catholic
  Primary School
  CHTN/BK PR9 ....**10** A3
Holy Trinity CE Primary
  School *CHTN/BK* PR9 ....**3** J2
Kensington Industrial Estate
  CHTN/BK PR9 ....**3** K5
Kew Medical Centre
  STHP PR8 ....**14** A2
Kew Retail Park
  STHP PR8 ....**14** C1
Kew Woods Primary School
  STHP PR8 ....**14** A2
King George V College
  STHP PR8 ....**10** A5
Kingsbury School
  ORM L39 ....**26** C5
Kings Meadow Primary
  School *STHP* PR8 ....**19** F5
Kingswood College at
  Scarisbrick School
  BRSC L40 ....**21** E2
Larkfield Primary School
  CHTN/BK PR9 ....**5** G4
Lathom High School
  SKEL WN8 ....**33** E2
Linaker Primary School
  STHP PR8 ....**9** F5
Lincoln Road Health Centre
  STHP PR8 ....**13** E4
Little Digmoor Primary School
  SKEL WN8 ....**37** G2
Little Theatre
  CHTN/BK PR9 ....**3** H3
Lordsgate Township CE
  Primary School
  BRSC L40 ....**23** F3
Marble Place Shopping Centre
  STHP PR8 ....**3** G4
Marshside Primary School
  CHTN/BK PR9 ....**5** F2
Marshside RSPB Reserve
  CHTN/BK PR9 ,,...............................**4** D2
Mayflower Industrial Estate
  FMBY L37 ....**29** G5
Meols Cop High School
  STHP PR8 ....**10** B5
Meols Cop Retail Park
  CHTN/BK PR9 ....**14** B1
Merefield Special School
  STHP PR8 ....**18** D4
Metropole Hotel
  STHP PR8 ....**3** F5
Model Village
  STHP PR8 ....**3**
Moorside Primary School
  SKEL WN8 ....**38** B1
Mount Carmel Preparatory
  School *ORM* L39 ....**30** C3
North Meols Community
  Leisure Centre
  CHTN/BK PR9 ....**7** F2
North Meols Lawn Tennis Club
  CHTN/BK PR9 ....**10** C1
Norwood Primary School
  CHTN/BK PR9 ....**10** A3
Nye Bevan Swimming Pool
  SKEL WN8 ....**33** G4
Old Hall Farm Business Park
  CHTN/BK PR9 ....**10** C5

Ormskirk Business Park
  ORM L39 ....**27** E4
Ormskirk CE Primary School
  ORM L39 ....**27** E4
Ormskirk College
  ORM L39 ....**26** D4
Ormskirk CC
  ORM L39 ....**31** E1
Ormskirk & District General
  Hospital *ORM* L39 ....**31** E1
Ormskirk Rugby Union FC
  ORM L39 ....**26** D4
Ormskirk School
  ORM L39 ....**27** G5
Orrell Clinic
  WGNW/BIL/OR WN5 ....**39** H1
Orrell Holgate Primary School
  WGNW/BIL/OR WN5 ....**39** H3
Orrell Newfold Community
  Primary School
  WGNW/BIL/OR WN5 ....**39** G4
Orrell RUFC
  WGNW/BIL/OR WN5 ....**39** H3
Orrell Water Park
  WGNW/BIL/OR WN5 ....**39** H4
Our Lady of Compassion RC
  Primary School
  FMBY L37 ....**29** G3
Our Lady of Lourdes RC Primary
  School *STHP* PR8 ....**13** E4
Our Lady Queen of Peace
  Catholic High School
  BRSC L40 ....**33** E1
Park Pool
  ORM L39 ....**26** D5
Peterhouse School
  CHTN/BK PR9 ....**5** H4
Pinfold Primary School
  BRSC L40 ....**20** D5
Platts Lane Industrial Estate
  BRSC L40 ....**23** F5
Pleasureland
  STHP PR8 ....**2** C3
Pontville School
  ORM L39 ....**30** C2
Premier Travel Inn
  STHP PR8 ....**2** E1
Presfield Special School
  CHTN/BK PR9 ....**5** G4
Quality Hotel
  SKEL WN8 ....**38** C3
Queenscourt Hospice
  STHP PR8 ....**14** A1
Redgate Primary School
  FMBY L37 ....**29** G4
Ringtail Industrial Estate
  BRSC L40 ....**22** C5
Riverside Holiday Park
  CHTN/BK PR9 ....**7** H4
Roby Mill CE Primary School
  SKEL WN8 ....**35** E2
Rosehill Business Park
  CHTN/BK PR9 ....**9** H4
The Royal Birkdale Golf Club
  STHP PR8 ....**12** B4
St Annes RC Primary School
  ORM L39 ....**30** C1
St Bedes Catholic High
  School *ORM* L39 ....**30** C1
St Edmunds Catholic Primary
  School *SKEL* WN8 ....**33** E4
St Francis of Assisi Catholic
  Primary School
  SKEL WN8 ....**38** A1

St James Catholic
  Primary School
  WGNW/BIL/OR WN5 ....**39** G4
St James RC Primary School
  SKEL WN8 ....**33** G1
St Johns Catholic
  Primary School
  BRSC L40 ....**23** F5
St Johns CE Primary School
  BRSC L40 ....**23** G2
  CHTN/BK PR9 ....**6** A2
St Johns RC Primary School
  SKEL WN8 ....**33** H4
St John Stone Catholic
  Primary School
  STHP PR8 ....**25** F1
St Lukes CE Primary School
  FMBY L37 ....**28** D5
St Marks CE Primary School
  BRSC L40 ....**15** F5
St Marys RC Primary School
  BRSC L40 ....**21** E1
St Patricks RC Primary School
  CHTN/BK PR9 ....**5** G5
St Peters CE Primary School
  FMBY L37 ....**29** G1
St Philips CE Primary School
  STHP PR8 ....**3** K6
St Richards Catholic
  Primary School
  SKEL WN8 ....**32** B4
St Stephens CE Primary School
  CHTN/BK PR9 ....**7** E2
St Teresas Catholic
  Primary School
  SKEL WN8 ....**35** E4
St Teresas RC Infant School
  STHP PR8 ....**13** E1
St Thomas the Martyr CE
  Primary School
  SKEL WN8 ....**39** E1
Sandy Lane Health Centre
  SKEL WN8 ....**32** C4
Scarisbrick Hotel
  STHP PR8 ....**3** F3
Shaw Hall Caravan Park
  BRSC L40 ....**21** F4
Shoreside Primary School
  STHP PR8 ....**18** D4
Shorrocks Hill Country Club
  FMBY L37 ....**28** B5
Skelmersdale & Ormskirk
  College (Northway Centre)
  SKEL WN8 ....**33** F4
Skelmersdale & Ormskirk
  College (Westbank Centre)
  SKEL WN8 ....**33** F5
Skelmersdale Sports Centre
  SKEL WN8 ....**37** H1
Skelmersdale United FC
  SKEL WN8 ....**32** B5
Slaidburn Industrial Estate
  CHTN/BK PR9 ....**5** G3
Southbank Tennis Club
  STHP PR8 ....**14** A1
Southport & Ainsdale
  Golf Club
  STHP PR8 ....**19** E2
Southport & Birkdale CC
  STHP PR8 ....**12** C2
Southport Business Centre
  CHTN/BK PR9 ....**3** H3
Southport Business Park
  STHP PR8 ....**13** E2

Southport College of
  Further Education
  CHTN/BK PR9 ....**3**
Southport Crematorium
  STHP PR8 ....**14**
Southport FC
  ....**10**
Southport Flower Show Site
  ....**2**
Southport & Formby District
  General Hospital
  STHP PR8 ....**14**
Southport & Formby Hospital
  CHTN/BK PR9 ....**3**
Southport General Infirmary
  STHP PR8 ....**9**
Southport Girls FC
  ....**10**
Southport Landing Area
  STHP PR8 ....**8**
Southport Municipal Golf Club
  CHTN/BK PR9 ....**4**
Southport Old Links Golf Club
  CHTN/BK PR9 ....**10**
Southport Pier
  STHP PR8 ....**8**
Southport RFC
  ....**12**
Southport Sailing Club
  STHP PR8 ....**9**
Southport Swimming Baths
  STHP PR8 ....**2**
Sphynx Tennis Club
  STHP PR8 ....**14**
The Sporting Edge Track
  ORM L39 ....**31**
Stanley High School Specialist
  Sports College
  CHTN/BK PR9 ....**5**
Sunnymede School
  STHP PR8 ....**2**
Theatre & Floral Hall
  CHTN/BK PR9 ....**3**
Trinity Primary School
  SKEL WN8 ....**32**
Up Holland High School
  WGNW/BIL/OR WN5 ....**39**
West End Primary School
  ORM L39 ....**26**
West Gillbrands Industrial
  Estate
  SKEL WN8 ....**36**
West Lancashire Yacht Club
  STHP PR8 ....**9**
Whiteledge Centre
  SKEL WN8 ....**33**
Wildfowl & Wetlands Trust
  Martin Mere
  BRSC L40 ....**17**
Willowbank Holiday Home &
  Touring Park
  STHP PR8 ....**24**
Windmill Animal Farm
  BRSC L40 ....**17**
Winstanley College
  WGNW/BIL/OR WN5 ....**39**
Woodland Primary School
  SKEL WN8 ....**33**
Woodlands Primary School
  FMBY L37 ....**28**
Woodvale Airfield
  FMBY L37 ....**24**

Acknowledgements

Schools address data provided by Education Direct.

Petrol station information supplied by Johnsons.

Garden centre information provided by:

Garden Centre Association  Britains best garden centres

Wyevale Garden Centres

The statement on the front cover of this atlas is sourced, selected and quoted from a reader comment and feedback form received in 2004

 **Street by Street** QUESTIONNAIRE

Dear Atlas User
Your comments, opinions and recommendations are very important to us.
So please help us to improve our street atlases by taking a few minutes
to complete this simple questionnaire.

You do not need a stamp (unless posted outside the UK). If you do not want to remove
this page from your street atlas, then photocopy it or write your answers on a plain sheet
of paper.

Send to: Marketing Assistant, AA Publishing, 14th Floor Fanum House,
Freepost SCE 4598, Basingstoke RG21 4GY

ABOUT THE ATLAS...

Please state which city / town / county you bought:

_____

Where did you buy the atlas? (City, Town, County)

_____

For what purpose? (please tick all applicable)

To use in your local area ☐   **To use on business or at work** ☐

Visiting a strange place ☐   **In the car** ☐   **On foot** ☐

Other (please state)

_____

Have you ever used any street atlases other than AA Street by Street?

Yes ☐   **No** ☐

If so, which ones?

_____

Is there any aspect of our street atlases that could be improved?
(Please continue on a separate sheet if necessary)

_____

_____

_____

ML202z

continued overleaf

Please list the features you found most useful:

_____

_____

Please list the features you found least useful:

_____

_____

_____

LOCAL KNOWLEDGE... ○   ○

Local knowledge is invaluable. Whilst every attempt has been made to make the information contained in this atlas as accurate as possible, should you notice any inaccuracies, please detail them below (if necessary, use a blank piece of paper) or e-mail us at _streetbystreet@theAA.com_

_____

_____

_____

ABOUT YOU...

Name (Mr/Mrs/Ms) _____

Address _____

Postcode _____

Daytime tel no _____

E-mail address _____

Which age group are you in?

Under 25 ☐   **25-34** ☐   **35-44** ☐   **45-54** ☐   **55-64** ☐   **65+** ☐

Are you an AA member?   YES ☐   **NO** ☐

Do you have Internet access?   YES ☐   **NO** ☐

Thank you for taking the time to complete this questionnaire. Please send it to us as soon as possible, and remember, you do not need a stamp (unless posted outside the UK).

We may use information we hold about you to, telephone or email you about other products and services offered by the AA, we do NOT disclose this information to third parties.

Please tick here if you do not wish to hear about products and services from the AA. ☐

ML202z ✂